Women Writing Nature

Women Writing Nature

A Feminist View

EDITED BY
BARBARA J. COOK

LEXINGTON BOOKS

A division of
ROWMAN & LITTLEFIELD PUBLISHERS, INC.
Lanham • Boulder • New York • Toronto • Plymouth, UK

LEXINGTON BOOKS

A division of Rowman & Littlefield Publishers, Inc.
A wholly owned subsidiary of The Rowman & Littlefield Publishing Group, Inc.
4501 Forbes Boulevard, Suite 200
Lanham, MD 20706

Estover Road
Plymouth PL6 7PY
United Kingdom

British Library Cataloguing in Publication Information Available

Library of Congress Cataloging-in-Publication Data

Women writing nature : a feminist view / edited by Barbara J. Cook.
p. cm.
Includes bibliographical references and index.
ISBN-13: 978-0-7391-1912-9 (cloth : alk. paper)
ISBN-10: 0-7391-1912-5 (cloth : alk. paper)
ISBN-13: 978-0-7391-1913-6 (pbk. : alk. paper)
ISBN-10: 0-7391-1913-3 (pbk. : alk. paper)
1. American literature—Women authors—History and criticism. 2. Natural history literature. 3. Ecofeminism in literature. 4. Philosophy of nature in literature. 5. Feminism and literature. 6. Feminist criticism. 7. Ecocriticism. I. Cook, Barbara J.
PS163.W66 2008
810.9'36—dc22 2007038882

Printed in the United States of America

∞™ The paper used in this publication meets the minimum requirements of American National Standard for Information Sciences—Permanence of Paper for Printed Library Materials, ANSI/NISO Z39.48–1992.

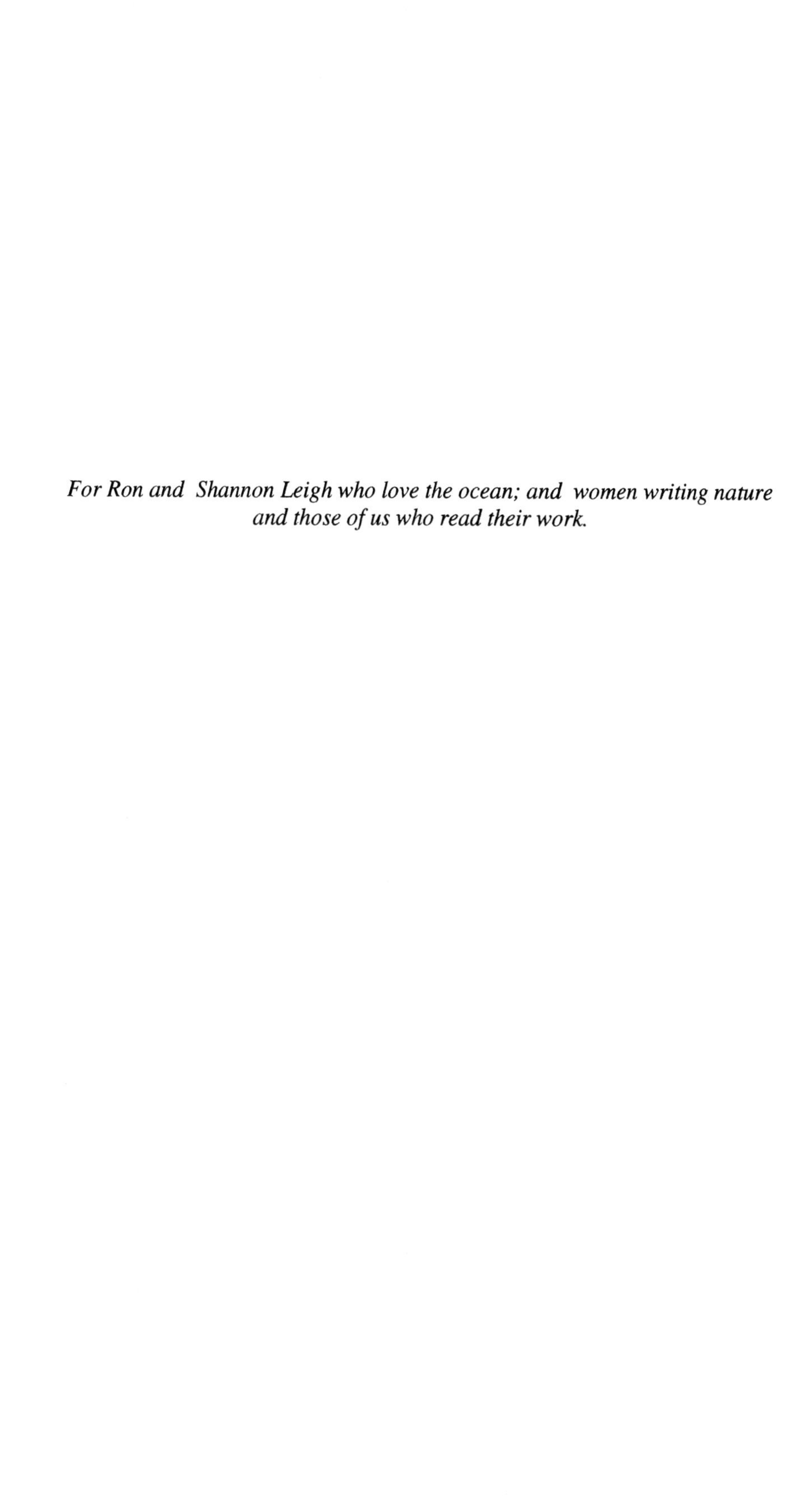

For Ron and Shannon Leigh who love the ocean; and women writing nature and those of us who read their work.

Table of Contents

Voices From the Field

1

Introduction: Nature Writing from the Feminine

Barbara J. Cook

Rachel Carson, writer, scientist, and ecologist, became famous as a naturalist and science writer for the public. Embedded in her early works was the view that human beings were but one part of nature distinguished primarily by their power to alter it, in some cases irreversibly. With the 1962 publication of *Silent Spring*, she challenged the practices of agricultural scientists and the government, and called for a change in the way humankind viewed the natural world.[1]

Since *Silent Spring* was published, the number of texts about the natural world written by women has grown exponentially. These fiction and nonfiction texts are as diverse as the women who write them. Terry Tempest Williams draws connections between cancer in her extended family and the downwind effect of nuclear testing. Kathleen Dean Moore links her exploration of rivers and Pacific coastal bays to an understanding of her father and her children. Susan Griffin explores the eroticism of the natural world. Writers such as Ana Castillo and Linda Hogan call attention to environmental justice issues and the effects on minority communities.

These women are utilizing the historical connection of women and the natural world in new ways as the essays in this volume argue. For centuries women have been associated with nature but many feminists have sought to distance themselves from nature because of the representations of women controlled by powerful Anatural forces@ and confined to domestic spaces.[2] However, in the spirit of Rachel Carson, some writers have begun to invoke nature for feminist purposes or have used nature as an agent of resistance. Drawing on the feminist tradition of the importance of the plurality of voices, each of the critical essays in *Women Writing Nature* addresses, although often in contradictory ways, the historical links between women and the natural world and the resistance tactics used by these women writing about the natural world. One of the questions that Cheryl Glotfelty asked in the *The Ecocriticism Reader*, was whether women write about nature differently than men.[3] This volume, which grew out of a roundtable discussion at a Northeastern Modern Language conference (NEMLA), is an attempt to answer that question. Although, since Glotfelty's groundbreaking collection of essays, there have been many essays in journals and other collections that address the writing of women authors from an eco-critical perspective, this project considers women=s writings about the natural world in light of recent and current feminist and ecofeminist theory. As will become apparent in these essays, there are a variety of approaches and applications of these theories. The definitions within feminist thought, especially ecofeminist thought, have shifted and changed over the years. Most scholars associate the term ecofeminist with French feminist, Françoise d'Eaubonne, but some scholars point to Carolyn Merchant's groundbreaking text, *Death of Nature* as foundational to current scholarship. As Susan Rosen points out, even the roots of ecofeminism are slippery.

In addition to focusing on feminist approaches, it is important to consider texts by women that may not have received the attention they deserve. Again, this is an effort to include a plurality of voices. Although some of our contributors discuss writers such as Rachel Carson and Terry Tempest Williams, this project seeks to move past these and other foundational writers such as Susan Griffin. The women discussed in this collection range from early writers such as the Taos group of the 1920s to the mid 1950s reflections of Anne Morrow Lindbergh to more recent writing. Though more attention needs to be given to women outside the Anglo American nature writing tradition than this volume provides, there is an essay on Canadian Margaret Atwood and one on Chicana writer Ana Castillo. The collection culminates with the voices of two women who write the natural world from a feminist perspective, one an American scientist, academic, and activist, one an Irish poet. Many of the scholars and their subjects are activists and academics. All point to the possibility of linking theory and practice, essential in feminist thought.

In the first essay, "Modernist Women, Snake Stories, and the Indigenous Southwest: An Ecofeminist Politics of Creation and Affirmation," Alex Hunt argues that female modernist writers who traveled to the southwest should be considered early ecofeminists. Although each woman had her own individual perspectives and artistic goals, "collectively, they pursued a political vision" which "sought to elevate and defend woman, natives, and the natural world." His essay explores the way in which the work of Mabel Dodge Luhan, Willa Cather, Mary Austin, and Alice Corbin made use of "Pueblo ideas to reimagine their own Judeo-Christian heritage." Within the desert landscape of the American Southwest, each woman reimagined the Garden of Eden and the serpent's role in the fall. Hunt finds that through the study of indigenous creation stories in the Southwest, these Modernist writers create their own revisions of the "legacy of Eve's fall." These revisions can be seen as engaging with ecofeminist philosopher Val Plumwood's project of challenging Western traditional concepts of dichotomy—male/female, reason/unreason.

Although these writers have been occasionally criticized for the appropriation of Native American stories and traditions, Hunt makes a strong case that their literary imaginations reveal human connections to nature rather than separation from nature and that within their work we can find elements of the ecofeminist work later women writers are engaged in.

There were other writers who foreshadowed contemporary ecofeminism. For instance, two mid-twentieth century nature writers, Anne Morrow Lindbergh and Rachel Carson, writing within the social and political constraints of the 1950s, focused on sea and coastal spaces. And, in "Littoral Women Writing from the Margins," Susan Rosen points to the importance of their writings which focus on the margins inherent in coastal lands and the connections of those margins to women's circumstances. Carson and Lindbergh, along with other women writing about the coast, "consistently integrated observations of nature with connections to their lower status in society or to their awareness that the coast could be extended, through metaphor, to reflect domestic issues, environmental issues, societal issues." Their work serves as a model for more recent nature writers such as Jennifer Ackerman and Mary Parker Buckles who fifty years later become part of an emerging tradition in women's coastal writing. They blend perspectives from literature, science, sociology, philosophy, history, environmentalism, and religion in order to understand the shifting margins of their own lives.

Kathleen Dean Moore also writes about coastal regions and rivers but her focus is the Pacific Northwest coastal region. In "Multifaceted Dialogues: Toward an Environmental Ethic of Care," I argue that Moore, a philosopher, draws on recent work in feminist moral theory and places the outdoors in dialogue not only with self but with our families, our relationships, our lives." In her essays, Moore is not alone in the wilderness, she "blends experience and observation, with knowledge and science and with memory and personal life." Moore's philosophical musings lead her to examine what it means for humanity to encompass an environmental ethic of care; thus extending the ethical boundaries of Aldo Leopold's foundational call for a land ethic beyond what some feminist scholars have called an ethic rooted in an heroic notion of ethical conduct as restraint of aggression"[4].

Sarah E. McFarland questions the traditional notion that the wilderness is "no place for women." She argues that American nature writing, most often a male construct, grew from the roots of exploration. In "Wild Women: Literary Explorations of American Landscapes," McFarland examines works by Susan Zwinger and Terry Tempest Williams and argues their writing challenges traditional stereotypes about "landscape, women, animals, and nature exploration." Their interactions with the natural world "resist the erasure of women from wilderness."

Although Zwinger acknowledges her own animal nature, she is aware of the negative aspects of the long association of women with nature. Her writing depicts the individual nature of the animals she encounters while at the same time describes how her own sense of the natural world changes and adapts. The connections Williams draws between the birds she writes about in *Refuge* and herself and her family are more problematic depictions. Both Zwinger and Williams disrupt, to varying degrees, the view of animals as other; thus, providing space for the agency of women's "animalness."

Mary Kate Azcuy's close reading of Louise Gluck's three part poem, "The Egg," moves from the outdoors to Gluck's personal bodily experience and her personal struggle to come to terms with those experiences. In "Louise Gluck, Feminism and Nature in *Firstborn*'s 'The Egg,'" Azcuy proposes the questions and answers that she argues define Gluck's lifelong search for "understanding of and relationship to the environment and the mythic as she redefines feminine via detailed, poetic landscape images." In her essay, Azcuy points to complex metaphors linked to Earth, creation, and recreation and personal struggle. In making her argument, Azcuy draws on French feminist theory which often reflect the roots of ecofeminist thought and shows that as Gluck works through her personal demons in this poem, she moves away from traditional spirituality and a patriarchal God toward the feminine in the natural world.

One of the key tenets of ecofeminist thought is the parallel between man's domination of nature and the exploitation and oppression of women. Recently, attention is being paid to the exploitation and oppression of the Other, people of color and the underclass. In "Ecofeminism, Motherhood, and the Post-Apocalyptic Utopia in *Parable of the Sower*, *Parable of the Talents*, and *Into the Forest*," Heidi Hutner proposes that these novels by Octavia Butler and Jean Hegland "attempt to solve the problem of ecological devastation and the oppression of women [and other Others] with the creation of utopian feminized societies based on what Carolyn Merchant calls an egalitarian 'partnership ethic' between the 'human community and nonhuman nature.'" Hutner argues that essentialized motherhood/nurturing is called into question by Butler and Hegland when the mothers in these novel are "distanced from the natural environment and their children." Butler's protagonist seemingly chooses to nuture her utopian community rather than her child. These actions result in loss of her daughter and, ultimately, when reunited later in life, alienation. Hegland also portrays disruption of traditional motherhood roles, a disruption resulting from the degradation of the earth and her resources.

Ecofeminist scholarship has disproportionately focused on American women's writing, most often white women. However, Canadian writer Margaret Atwood's early novel, *Surfacing*, has received much attention even though many scholars have found it problematic from an ecofeminist perspective. Some have observed that her female characters appear to invade and use nature in much the same way that men use both nature and women. H. Louise Davis extends this debate regarding the ecofeminist dimensions of Atwood's work in "Natural Resistance: Margaret Atwood as Ecofeminist or Apocalyptic Visionary." Davis proposes that much of Atwood's work contributes to the ecofeminist movement. Although her work is, as Atwood herself states, fictional stories and not political treatises, they do "raise questions about the role of all humans and implicate the reader in the subordination of women and nature and, in raising awareness of said subordination, [thus,] she enters into a dialogue about the plight of women and the environment."

Davis finds elements ecofeminist elements in Atwood's poetry and short stories and believes that the 2004 novel, *Oryx and Crake* makes a significant shift toward an ecofeminist stance. Ironically, in this novel, Atwood's protagonist is male rather than the female character she usually writes about. In Atwood's work, there is a sense that nature and culture are not separate and that human and nature interaction has consequences. Davis proposes that *Oryx* successfully expands the definition of ecofeminisn.

In "Touching the Earth: Gloria Anzaldúa and the Tenets of Ecofeminism," Allison Steele draws our attention to Chicana writer Gloria Anzaldúa's role in calling for a revision of the patriarchally derived stories and myths we find throughout the Western world. In doing so, Anzaldúa draws on borderland myths and provides examples of connections of Chicanas/os, "border people," and the Earth. In interviews and her writings, "Anzaldúa effectively creates a space for Chicana feminists to have a voice and a story" within the ecofeminist movement as they rewrite these oppressive myths. Steele argues that "Rewriting culture and allowing space for the pens of other Chicana feminists is Anzaldúa's radically active gift to ecofeminism." She finds that Anzaldúa responds to critiques by social construction ecofeminists who seem to deny nature as an entity. Anzaldúa's call for Chicanas to take action to defend the natural world speaks to all ecofeminist activists.

The second section of this collection, "Voices From the Field," features the meditations of two women nature writers. These two chapters are not about women nature writers, rather they are by women nature writers. The very different perspectives of these two writers aptly reflect the diversity to be found within any group of women who write about nature. Some of the issues addressed in their essays are: What does the experience of being a female nature writer feel like? How does our Western culture encourage or discourage women who write about nature? For these answers we must, and should, turn to the writers themselves who can tell us in the first person.

In "How to be a Female Nature Writer," scientist and environmentalist, Joan Maloof presents what she considers the nine keys to writing about nature. She urges potential writers to get up, go out, to be afraid to go alone into the wilderness, to read but not to try to read everything before writing and to look and question change. Finally, Maloof believes that nature writing should be about trying to save the world—she writes: "I think that trying to save some of this beautiful, complex, joyful, place is the most important work there is." As an activist and scientist, Maloof, has much in common with Rachel Carson. Both studied science in the university system and published papers in scientific journals, but eventually they turned to nature writing as a way to reach a larger audience. Maloof's book, *Teaching the Trees*, was published in 2005 by the University of Georgia Press. It is now in its fourth printing and was released as a paperback in 2007. As Maloof herself points out, both she and Carson "share a courageous, activist, attitude, and . . . [both] speak out to protect the world they know so well and love so dearly."

In "Confessions of an Ecofeminist," Irish poet Rosemarie Rowley takes us on her journey to ecofeminist consciousness beginning with her reading of Rachel Carson's 1962 book, *Silent Spring*. Written in both prose and poetry, Rowley's journey reflects the evolution of feminist and ecological thought in England and Ireland during the last half of the twentieth century. She connects her own often abusive, but mostly disappointing relationships with the degradation of the landscapes she loves.

This collection of essays offers the reader perspectives and texts as diverse as the women who write about the natural world. My intent is to continue the discussion initiated by Glotfelty's question, "Do women write about nature differently than men?" Most of the authors in this collection argue that they do, although the ways in which they differ from their male counterparts cannot be placed within a single monolithic category. However, I believe their work is a step toward answering Rachel Carson's call to change the way we view the natural world.

Notes

1. Linda Lear, "The Life and Legacy of Rachel Carson," Rachel Carson Home Page, 1998, http://www.rachelcarson.org (accessed April 16, 2006).

2. This historical connection is discussed at length in Carolyn Merchant, *Death of Nature: Women, Ecology and the Scientific Revolution* (New York: HarperCollins Publishers, 1980). Merchant argues that since the decline of women centered religions in the pre-modern world, societal forces grounded in the notion of reason and scientific method, have sought to connect women with the negative aspects of the natural world; thus, repressing both women and nature.

3. Cheryl Glotfelty, "Introduction: Literary Studies in an Age of Enviromental Crisis." *The Ecocriticism Reader.* Cheryll Glotfelty and Harold Fromm, eds. (Athens: University of Georgia Press, 1996), xix.

4. Marti Kheel, "From Heroic to Holistic Ethics: The Ecofeminist Challenge," *Ecofeminism: Women, Animals, Nature*. Greta Gaard, ed. (Philadelphia: Temple University Press, 1993), 251.

2

Modernist Women, Snake Stories, and the Indigenous Southwest: An Ecofeminist Politics of Creation and Affirmation

Alex Hunt

The common understanding of Eve's transgression in the Garden of Eden has long served to fuel Western cultural misogyny. Yielding to the serpent's temptation—to be God-like—Eve eats the fruit of the Tree of Knowledge of Good and Evil. She gives fruit to Adam, and he eats. In their new state of knowledge, they cover their nakedness. God curses the serpent, creating enmity between animal and human. He curses Eve with the pain of child birth and with subjection. Finally, God curses the land and curses Adam to labor for his sustenance. He further tells Adam that he will die and return to dust. And so, from a state of innocent grace in a perfect paradise of human dominion over nature in which man and God-the-father are in perfect understanding, as Milton teaches us, the woman blew it. Men have been punishing women and fighting to regain their earthly dominion ever since. If ecofeminism in its broadest definition concerns the connections between and common oppression of woman and nature, the Garden of Eden story is a very good place to critique and reinterpret our cultural legacy. As Carolyn Merchant puts it, "The Recovery of Eden story is . . . perhaps the most important mythology humans have developed to make sense of their relationship to the earth."[1] In examining this legacy, we should also remember that the Christian understanding of the story masks other more ancient analogues and more diverse creation stories.

One rich source for considering confluences of creation stories is through the writing of women Modernists who traveled to the Southwest—particularly the pueblo territories of New Mexico—in search of new ideas in what they perceived as primitive rhythms of indigenous America. In this essay I am interested in exploring use that Modernist women writers Mabel Dodge Luhan, Willa Cather, Mary Austin, and Alice Corbin made of Indigenous Pueblo ideas to reimagine their own Judeo-Christian heritage. Of these writers, I will comment in most detail on Cather's work, as it contains the most explicit and instructive critique, inspired by pueblo cosmology, of the Garden of Eden story. While each of the writers I'll consider had her own artistic goals and individual perspectives, they pursued similar philosophical and political visions. This is because they were reacting against similar antagonizing forces; Val Plumwood has noted that dominant ("white, western, male expert") forces in the western tradition have claimed reason and rationality as their purview, relegating women, colonial subjects, lower classes and nature as forces of unreason. Plumwood argues for the "redefinition or reconstruction of reason in less oppositional and hierarchical ways."[2] Modernist women in the Southwest, strongly feminist in their work and their lifestyles, were engaged with precisely this project.

The Anglo-feminist fascination with Puebloan cultures, while on the one hand a primitivist appropriation of indigenous cosmology in the name of a universal or archetypal feminine power, achieved an understanding that is a constructive common ground for indigenous, feminist, and environmentalist activists and scholars. My argument is that ultimately these women should be regarded as early ecofeminsts who engaged in constructive work that sought to elevate and defend woman, natives, and the natural world. As opposed to the rationalistic and scientistic view of reality that, as Plumwood suggests, was an instrumental part of the patriarchal culture they sought to escape, this new/primitivist vision celebrated a creative sense of a participatory reality rich in imaginative power and an affirmation of cultural difference, spiritual unity, and ecological connection.

What so intrigued these women about Puebloan indigenous cultures (Taos, Acoma, Tesuque, Hopi, Zuni, and others) was what they saw as their exotic, primitive difference. To their eyes, here was an ancient race in the midst of modernity, complete with its own cosmology and religious rites. Yet there existed just enough similarity between cultures (Jung traveled here hunting archetypes) that they found in pueblo cosmology potential for revision of their own; as we will see, there can be no doubt that these women were conscious of the Garden of Eden story as they wrote of the indigenous Southwest. No single Pueblo creation story that simply and neatly parallels Genesis, but in the diversity of these creation stories could be found alternatives—and perhaps antidotes—to the crippling legacy of Eve's fall. When Mabel Dodge Luhan, Willa Cather, Mary Austin, and other women writers and artists came to the Southwest, they found indigenous cultures that apparently operated by means of gynocentric or matriarchal models that seemed to offer emancipation from gender-oppression that was typical of their Victorian-era upbringing. Again, while these women were not immune from the pitfalls of the Euro-American tendency to appropriate indigenous primitive cultures for their own purposes, it is worth examining the creative affirmation of indigenous cultures that occurred here; in seeking an alternative to a scientific and patriarchal oppression of nature and woman, some progressive work of reimagining the earth took place. In short, these Modernist writers by turns found and constructed an alternative to the cultural legacy of Eve's fall in the Garden of Eden, a legacy that in many ways large and small conditioned their world and constrained their horizons.

A suggestive starting point, the serpent, is a powerfully charged iconographic figure for both Judeo-Christian and Puebloan cultures. As Robert Alter reminds us in his translation of Genesis, in its earliest sense "the serpent is by no means 'satanic,' as in the later Judeo-Christian traditions."[3] For Marija Gimbutas, scholar of European Archeology whose work includes the study of ancient Goddess mythology, there is clear evidence from the Paleolithic linking the serpent with the power of life-giving.[4] Furthermore, the snake is understood as "something primordial and mysterious, coming from the depths of the waters where life begins."[5] Significantly, Gimbutas notes that the snake was associated with the power of regeneration and fertility, and that its shape suggested the sinuosity and meanders of streams. She writes that snakes "must have been the guardians of the springs of life in prehistory, as they still are in European folklore."[6] This understanding bears comparison to Southwestern Puebloan cosmology.

Though particular stories and ceremonies vary, the snake is indeed an important deity for Pueblo peoples, associated with rainfall, springs, and rivers. The most important serpent deity is the Horned Water Serpent. Hamilton Tyler states that all snakes are messengers to the underground watery realms of the Horned Water Serpent: "Underneath the earth is a vast reservoir of water which rises to the surface in springs and lakes and rivers. The Horned Water Serpent is god of these lower waters"[7] Gutiérrez finds even greater complexity in this deity, who "united the vertical levels of the cosmos" in that he "combined the masculine germinative forces of the sky (rain) with the feminine generative power of the earth (seeds)." The Horned Water Serpent "provided the Pueblo Indians with fecundity and abundance by joining together the levels of the cosmos (sky/earth, earth/underworld) and social existence (male/female, life/death)."[8] In Pueblo ceremonial imagery, falling rain and striking lightening are figured as serpents. Rivers, especially as canyons seen from above, have meanders and curves suggestive of the sinuous serpent as well. Leslie Marmon Silko, in her discussion of the serpent, called "Ma'sh'ra'tru'ee" in Laguna Pueblo tradition, also notes that springs were marked with petroglyphs of coiled snakes whose heads pointed toward the spring.[9] Rather than carrying Christian connotations of sin, evil, and Satan, connotations which also link woman to transgression, Pueblo snake traditions—no less connected to the matter of life and creation—offer a compelling vision of woman and nature.

Indeed, Anglo modernist women found very different and compelling ideas of gender, sexuality, and nature in the indigenous Southwest. Historian Ramón Gutiérrez explains in *When Jesus Came, the Corn Mothers Went Away: Marriage, Sexuality, and Power in New Mexico* that in indigenous Pueblo society, women were as powerful as men, in a balance that was enacted in all aspects of social custom. Women's power was that of the home and garden, their nurturance and their sexuality. Women's life-giving ability was analogous to that of the earth that produced corn after a rain. Sexuality was thus empowering, and sexual behavior openly celebrated. Gutiérrez finds that in unambiguous ways, "Sexuality was equated with fertility, regeneration, and the holy by the Pueblo Indians."[10] This unfallen sense of the feminine, sexuality, and nature suggests a path to re-interpreting the Garden of Eden.

It is often remarked that the Judeo-Christian tradition is conditioned by the fact that its stories emerged from arid country access to water and susceptibility to drought were bedrock conditions. Remember that when Adam and Eve, cursed and fallen, marked by the shame of their sexual bodies, must leave the garden, they wander into desert. From another desert, consider how refreshingly different Pueblo cosmologies emerged. Gutiérrez's account of Acoma creation stories emphasize the positive associations of sexuality and fertility in the desert: "The Acoma Indians say they were conceived when Pishuni, the serpentine deity of water, entered Nautsiti's body as rain. At the beginning of time, too, Thought Woman taught the Corn Mothers that maize would give them life if planted within Mother Earth's womb. When the clouds (men) poured down their rain (semen) the seeds (women) would germinate and come to life."[11] In this account, one can see that there can be no line drawn between human sexuality and the fertility of the land, no barrier between human behavior and the operations of the weather. The deity Pishuni, representing water, is associated with a sexual act, but there is no suggestion here of transgression. For those in search of new ideas in ancient cultures, here was evocative material.

Women Modernist writers in the Southwest responded energetically to Pueblo ideas of the landscape and the cosmos. Alice Corbin, whose poetry in her 1920 collection, *Red Earth: Poems of New Mexico*, demonstrates this energy and the desire affirm indigenous worldviews. Corbin's tuberculosis, which brought her to New Mexico in 1916, might have led her to see the desert as a place of harsh arid death. But instead she sees in the desert renewal and fecundity, an Edenic vision of a Primitivist poetics. Rejecting the "stream of money" that is "flowing down Fifth Avenue" in the poem "In the Desert," Corbin finds life flowing through the desert: "Nothing but life in the desert, / Intense life."[12] In the final section of the poem Corbin presents an image of the acequia system of New Mexico villages: "Willows along the acequias in the valley / Give cool streams of green; / Beyond, on the bare hillsides, / Yellow and red gashes and bleached white paths / Give foothold to the burros, / to the black-shawled Mexican girls / Who go for water."[13] In pueblo communities of the Southwest, the acequia system is the hydrological life-blood. Mountain melt-water is funneled to the "acequia madre" which is then divided to different villages and farms; that the association of woman and nature found in the Spanish was not lost on Corbin is clear from other poems in the collection.

In "From the Stone Age," for example, Corbin adopts the persona of a sentient, feminine earth. The poem begins, "Long age some one carved me in the semblance of a god. / I have forgotten now what god I was meant to represent."[14] Though this image was carved in stone, the speaker is only conscious of itself/herself as stone, stone body which "is the substance of life itself," and through which life flows, "Moving through my pores of stone." Self-consciousness continues to fade as the speaker concludes: "My body retains only faintly the image / It was meant to represent, / I am more beautiful and less rigid, / I am part of space, / Time has entered into me, Life has passed through me— / What matter the name of the god I was meant to represent?"[15] The earth as Goddess, though retaining sentience, requires no proper name, Corbin suggests; the essential nature of the earth goddess precedes names and is universal, available to whatever cultural representations and namings that will inevitably come.

Corbin develops an embodied erotics of landscape that anticipates later ecofeminist writers like Susan Griffin and Terry Tempest Williams. In "The Stone-Pine and Stream," the femininity of the landscape, and the very body of the poet's persona merge: "The stone-pine with green branches / Stands on the brink of the canyon, / The wind whispers in the tree— / The wind lifts my hair. / Water runs with a pattern of braided and woven music / Through the streams in the canyon— / My body flows like water through the stream in the canyon."[16] Through the course of the book, land, community, and feminine life-giving elements gather strength as the poet seems to gain understanding of the indigenous and Hispano cultures.

Corbin gives credit for the inspiration for her ideas in poetry that represents and celebrates indigenous ceremonial language. In a poem titled "Corn-Grinding Song," Corbin employs a modern free verse style to emphasize the poetic character of indigenous ceremony: "This way from the north / Comes the cloud, / Very blue, / and inside the cloud is the blue corn. / *How beautiful the cloud / Bringing corn of blue color!*"[17] And then, "Corn springs up / From the seed in the ground, / The cradled corn / by the sun is found / . . . Hid in the cloud / The wind brings rain / And the water-song / To the dust-parched plain . . . The dancers' feet / Echo the sound / As the drums grow faint / And the rain comes down."[18] This ceremony refutes a dichotomous view of reality between wilderness and civilization. Here, human culture is woven into the essence of natural processes, and natural processes are intimately connected with human ceremonial observance. In her notes that conclude the book Corbin acknowledges of "Corn-Grinding Song," that the text was given her by a Tesuque Pueblo woman named Canuto Suaza: "My rendering is as direct as possible."[19] Corbin's notes indicate her awareness that the collection of indigenous ceremonial texts is a sensitive matter, that care is required. While Corbin does not include a direct reference to or refutation of a Judeo-Christian ethos or the Garden of Eden story, her poetry certainly brings together familiar Pueblo spiritual elements of feminine divinity; a sentient, feminine earth; and life-giving waters—sky-borne, terrestrial, and subterranean.

In her fiction and nonfiction, Mary Austin was centrally concerned with the natural world and the human cultures of the Southwest, and the connections between human and natural communities. I am particularly interested for my current purposes in Austin's 1924 book of cultural geography and ethnography, a regional history that is at the same time a kind of spiritual writing of place called *The Land of Journey's Ending*. Again, Mary Austin is by turns praised and criticized for her identification with indigenous peoples, but it is clear that as an early ecofeminist she found in indigenous examples a reverence for a living and sacred natural world.

It is clear that Austin wished to challenge the Garden of Eden story, and her indigenist critique of Christianity is quite playful. Commenting on the origin of peach trees growing on Hopi land, Austin recounts reading a pamphlet by a "learned gentleman" who sets out "to prove that the Fruit of the Tree, which the Serpent plucked for Eve, was no apple, but a peach."[20] Austin finds this a pleasing idea: "Where else would it naturally come, if actually out of Eden, but to the only place left in the world where the great Snake is still a deity and has dances performed in his honor?"[21] Austin refers here to the snake dance performed at Hopi, a ceremony that fascinated Euro-Americans precisely because of their Christian interpretation of the serpent.

Describing elements of the symbolism of a Tanoan ceremony calling for rain, she writes,

> The earth is sentient, and if you dance for it, thrills and flushes with the power of ripening the harvest. The great spruce-tree is knowledgeable, its roots reach down to the six great springs of the earth, its tip touches the clouds. The thunder is a bird, the most majestic, whose wings are made of the dark cloud, whose feathers are clashing flakes of obsidian, in whose claws are serpent-darting arrows of the lightening.[22]

She goes on to explain key elements of snake imagery:

> Springs are sacred, and under the protection of a symbolic concept made out of the analogy of snakes to the zigzag lightening and the sinuous course of rivers, and the use of plumes to symbolize the bird-flight of prayers on their way to Those Above. Thus, a cleverly constructed effigy of the great snake having feathers growing out of his head has become the chief fetish of a desert people.[23]

The serpent is no symbol of evil, clearly, but one of water, the essence of life in the desert. Like Alice Corbin Henderson, Austin sees the relationships between land and people expressed in religious belief and social practices.

Moreover, Austin understood the significance of water in the Southwest to an impressive extent. Austin developed a theory of bioregionalism, of living in harmony with the natural limits of the land, in large part through her observations of indigenous peoples of the deserts. Heike Schaefer points out that because of her study of Pueblo culture in particular Austin "reconceptualized the Southwest as a region in which the integration of Native American, Hispanic, and European American cultures could produce a sustainable democratic

American society."[24] In *The Land of Journey's Ending* Austin makes clear that the need to understand properly the nature of water in the desert requires a re-imagining of the most deeply held myths. At the snake dance, Austin writes, one can share in a realization: "suddenly the story of the Snake and the Tree is touched with mystery more insightful than theologians, have been able to give it."[25] Such a realization makes possible Austin's lovely description of rainfall: "Then the checked mass [of stormclouds] begins to bellow for the wind, *Thona! thona!* the voice of Rain standing! Into its cavernous blueness the People of the Lightening send their serpent-darting arrows. Around the roots of the junipers the rain makes slithery yellow runnels; it gurgles in the acequias. The great Corn Plant rejoices."[26] I am always struck, in reading Austin's work, by its vitality. How different, in tone and possibility, from a scientific anthropologist like J. W. Fewkes, who wrote in 1894 an important book about the Hopi snake ceremony and managed the following dry and sterile conclusion: "It seems probable that the Snake Dance is a ceremony for rain, and since its beginning to its close, wherever we turn, there appear elements which point to this conclusion."[27] Literary artists—even in the mode of nonfiction writing—inspire imagination and consciousness rather than reporting the facts merely. Austin implicitly calls for a new divinity, a revised story of the Garden, a hybrid spirituality, that is necessary to adaptation and celebration of the Southwestern deserts.

Enter the mystic. Mabel Dodge Luhan wrote several books based on her time in Taos. Luhan—compared to Cather, Austin, and even Corbin—is little-read, but is recognized, appreciated primarily as Taos matriarch and muse. Visitors to her Southwestern literary and artistic salon included D. H. Lawrence, Georgia O'Keefe, and John Collier, who I'll discuss later. If Luhan's literary efforts are under appreciated today, her ideas certainly inspired those around her, writers and artists who she inspired to carry on her visionary work. According to her biographer, Lois Rudnick, Luhan "identified herself with Woman as earth mother, with the 'female' values of love, nurture, and intuition that she learned would regenerate society by inspiring its great male talents . . . This 'new' philosophy, however, placed Woman in a position where she was at once raised above and kept beneath Man—both literally and figuratively."[28] In two books, *Taos Winter* (1935) and *Edge of the Taos Desert* (1937), we have her memoirs of her psychological and spiritual development as she experiences the natural rhythms of season and the lifestyles of Taos.

Less explicit but no less playful than Austin, Luhan indicates her wish to revise the Garden of Eden story. In *Edge of the Taos Desert* Luhan describes the sight of her future (fourth) husband, Antonio Lujan of Taos Pueblo: "I lay there wishing I could see Tony, for I knew that, and only that, would help me. I longed for him. About four o'clock I heard a low singing outside in the garden, and there he was, sitting on the old garden bench under the apple tree."[29] For Mabel Dodge, they were indeed the neo-Adam and Eve, Indigenous and Euro-American. Luhan was a far less astute scholar of Native American beliefs and customs than Mary Austin, and indeed Luhan's role is perhaps more significant as that of muse than of author. But as a bold visionary, Luhan understood enough to fashion her own kind of psychological and ecological cosmic worldview around her New Mexico experience.

As Luhan deepens her relationship with the Pueblo man who would become her husband, she learns from him something of the indigenous view of landscape: it is a deeply feminine and sexually-charged landscape for Luhan, who is continually moved to describe the power of spring runoff from the sacred mountains which recharge the land and electrify all life. She is clearly taken by the ceremonialism of the Pueblo tribes, remarking that in ceremonies "they are giving back to earth and sun what they have received. In due time they will harvest it again, in wheat and corn, and fruit. The everlasting exchange goes on—between men and the earth, one and inseparable, but infinitely divisible."[30] In Mabel Dodge Luhan's example we find anticipated Barbara Kingsolver's scenes of love in the ruins in *Animal Dreams*, where Anasazi sites are the backdrop to trans-ethnic passion.

More than once Mabel goes with Tony to sacred places, especially two evocative landscapes, one a cave with a spring and a waterfall at the head of Arroyo Hondo, the other the well-known Blue Lake, a sacred spot to indigenous tribes of the region. In *Winter in Taos* she describes the lake as "the most mysterious thing I have ever seen in nature, having an unknown, impenetrable life of its own."[31] She goes on to describe it as the source of the creeks that run through and irrigate pueblo farms and the source of the acequia madre that provides for the farms of the hispano communities as well. In *Edge of the Taos Desert*, Mabel Dodge describes her first view of the lake like as a highly mystical moment of interpersonal exchange: "I looked and my heart stopped, for the face of the Lake gazed up at us. It was directly below, a pool of lambent burning blue. It smiled. It had life, it had conscious life. I knew it."[32] In addition to her experience of the lake itself, her sense of the waters that flow from there demonstrates her lack of rigorous thought concerning indigenous worlds. The waters flowed out of the lake, Luhan writes, "down the long decline of the canyon, turning, twisting, persisting upon its course until it came to Taos Valley, crossed it, fell into the Rio Grande, and ran down to the Gulf of Mexico where Indians like these drink it, and it binds them further into one flesh and blood."[33] The notion that all indigenous people are one, spiritually or otherwise, demonstrates the extent of Luhan's romantic or poetic abstraction of a far more complex historical reality. And yet, as an ecocentric vision, the idea of being bound into a single flesh of the substance of creation is imaginatively powerful.

If Mabel Dodge Luhan's view of the lake is rather cosmic, it is because the night before, she says to treat a fever, she has taken a dose of peyote, which proves a religious experience for her. She sees, among other things, "that there is no single equilibrium anywhere in existence, and that the meaning and essence of balance is that it depends upon neighboring organisms, one leaning upon the other, one touching another, reinforcing the whole, creating form and defeating chaos which is the hellish realm of unattached and unassimilated atoms."[34] This vision of the cosmos, as Mabel Dodge Luhan recreates the memory some years after the event, is on the one hand impossibly abstract and hallucinatory, but on the other a vision of ecological harmony. It seems to me to articulate nature not only as the feminine source of life-nurturing waters but the spiritual source, too, of artistic creative power. From these experiences in the visionary and sexual power of the landscape came Luhan's idea of the Southwest as the center of a new artistic consciousness.

Even the far more level-headed and successful professional writer, Willa Cather, was not immune from the Southwest's exotic and inspirational textures. In *Death Comes for the Archbishop*, from 1927, Cather succeeds far better than her contemporaries, I think, in creating a unified or coherent vision of the Southwest as a site of a kind of ecofeminist politics. Cather found a source in a history of the Catholic church in New Mexico written by William Howlett, which she read while visiting Santa Fe in 1925. For readers who are accustomed to and interested in Cather's focus on women, *Death Comes for the Archbishop* seems an oddity, since it follows the lives of two historical churchmen, French missionary priests, Lamy and Machebeuf, renamed in the novel Latour and Vaillant.

In order to understand properly Cather's intention, one must see the parallel between Catholic clergy, who exist without heterosexual conventions of romance and marriage, and Cather herself, who never married. Cather's probable lesbianism aside, her choice of considering the close life-long friendship between two priests enables her to escape from conventional heterosexual plots and sentiments that were the standard fare of the novel. More than simply freeing her from the romantic plot, however, her choice of subject allows her an unexpected opening to explore quite unfamiliar ideas concerning gender and nature.

And yet, we are once again back in the Garden of Eden, or more properly, the even more ancient garden upon which the biblical story is based. Cather invokes the Garden of Eden story frequently with the novel's paradisical imagery and secret gardens. On one of Archbishop Latour's last trips into the country, visiting Canyon de Chelly, he reflects that even through all the upheavals of its colonial history, the place is like "an Indian Garden of Eden."[35] Ultimately Cather seeks ecofeminist origin stories more ancient than Genesis, a feminine earth that Latour cannot fully affirm though he comes to respect indigenous worldviews.

On one level, as we are engaged with Latour's efforts to administer the church, Cather's novel is an exploration of certain Pueblo ideas relating to gender and landscape. Latour travels with a young man of Pecos Pueblo named Jacinto. The Pecos people—though outwardly converted—maintain their religious customs; they are rumored to have a giant snake, their god, hidden in a secret cave. Naturally, there are rumors that the people make human sacrifices to the serpent. In their travels, when Latour and Jacinto are caught in a dangerous snowstorm, they take refuge in a hidden cave to which Jacinto rather uncomfortably takes the Catholic bishop. The entrance to the cavern is described as "two rounded ledges, one directly over the other, with a mouthlike opening between. They suggested two great stone lips, slightly parted and thrust outward." The two men "mount" the ledge and enter "through the orifice, into the throat of the cave."[36] In the back of this ceremonial cavern is another orifice of "an irregular oval shape" as large as "a very large watermelon."[37] Jacinto quickly closes this opening with stones and mud for plaster, concealing something beyond from Latour—and from the reader; Cather seems to respect a degree of secrecy regarding indigenous religious practice. The father is overcome by a "fetid odour" in the cavern, and also disturbed by a sound that seems to him "an extraordinary vibration in this cavern; it hummed like a hive of bees, like a heavy roll of distant drums."[38] When Latour complains of this disorienting sensation, Jacinto has the reverend father put his ear to a fissure in the stone floor. Cather writes:

> [Latour] told himself he was listening to one of the oldest voices of the earth. What he heard was the sound of a great underground river, flowing through a resounding cavern. The water was far, far below, perhaps as deep as the foot of the mountain, a flood moving in utter blackness under ribs of antediluvian rock. It was not a rushing noise, but the sound of a great flood moving with majesty and power.[39]

We are left to understand, though Cather does not connect the dots, that the underground river is the reality of the reported giant snake-god of the Pecos people. When Latour and Jacinto emerge from the cavern the next day, in case we missed the vagina and womb imagery running through the scene, the two "crawled out through the stone lips, and dropped into a gleaming white world" of "virgin snow," symbolically reborn.[40]

Indeed, in the arid Southwest, the water beneath the mountain is the ultimate spring, the source of life, and absolutely sacred. The story of human sacrifices to a huge snake that lives in a cave goes back at least to Charles Lummis' recounting of it. His dismissal as "foolish fable" of the gruesome tales of infant sacrifices, though, is undercut by his claim that Isleta Pueblo kept a massive "sacred rattler" in a nearby volcanic cave until it escaped five years earlier.[41] While Austin also makes mention of and dismisses this tale, Cather is the first writer to connect snakes, underground water, and divinity in such a fully imagined scene.

Latour's spiritual rebirth is not immediately profound; in fact he is quite horrified by the feminine power of the cavern. He—and the organized faith he represents—cannot handle the essence of the earth goddess. Still, by the end of the novel, by the time death comes for the archbishop, he at least respects the divinity of indigenous peoples; he sees, for example, his Navajo friend Eusabio—a character known to be modeled on Mabel's husband—who moves fluidly across the landscape as though he were a part of if rather than opposed to it. Latour thinks that "Travelling with Eusabio was like traveling with the landscape make human."[42] He further reflects that the indigenous way of "accommodating themselves" to a landscape was a spiritual practice of respect for nature that is admirable when opposed to the European need to "'master' nature, to arrange and re-create."[43]

Cather also succeeds in putting the Pueblo idea of the feminine earth into the larger context of deep history. Father Latour reflects on the miracle of the Virgin of Guadalupe as a particular blessing from god to the indigenous poor of Mexico. Both the Virgin of Guadalupe of Mexican and New Mexican Catholics and the Feminine spiritualism of the Puebloan tribes are, for Bishop Latour, consistent with the most ancient of divinities. He sits at a spring in the middle of a desert and thinks of other such places, "older than history" including "those well-heads in his own country where the Roman settlers had set up the image of a river goddess, and later the Christian priests had planted a cross" (32). For the enlightened Latour, divinity knows various manifestations, and these are perhaps accretive rather than exclusive. Nearing his death, the now-Archbishop Latour reflects upon the restoration of the Navajo to their ancestral lands, and seems to accept the fact that Navajo people need their landscapes, which are where divinity lives for them; their land is their mother, who protects her people.

Considered in terms of an ecofeminist politics, these Modernist women writers' accomplishment is not unproblematic. Not surprisingly, in revising and reclaiming the Eden story in their own literary constructions of the Southwest, these writers return to Romantic tropes that evoke the indigenous figure as the denizen and caretaker—whether pure or corrupted of the garden. Without question, this is a colonial trope which risks alignment with a masculine discourse of conquest, and its use by Luhan and others should not go unquestioned. Indeed, a number of scholars have found Anglo appropriations of the Southwest and the Native troubling, noting the tendency of Modern artists to construct the indigenous peoples in terms of a lost golden age rather than their contemporary realities. Audrey Goodman, to cite a compelling critique along these lines, considers the work of Anglo writers in the Southwest between 1880 and 1930 as demonstrating "dreams of translation" and "fascination with the dead and inaccessible" that does "violence to the living" and raises questions of whether outsiders can really "imagine native points of view."[44] Goodman's point is well-taken, yet it would be unfortunate if the work of women writers marginalized in a male-dominated canon and recently brought back to critical attention were summarily dismissed on the grounds of cultural misappropriation. Without denying the problem, we should consider what these women Modernists did achieve in the work—a richly reimagined world of the spiritual, the feminine, and the ecological.

Nor should we forget that Mabel Dodge Luhan and Mary Austin, especially, were attuned to the political realities of the Pueblos and made political activism a crucial part of their work. These writers made good-faith efforts to understand and affirm ethnic and cultural difference. They were no doubt products of their time, and as such reflected attitudes such as that of the influential anthropologist Franz Boas, whose work in collecting indigenous stories carried the tacit under standing that these cultures were tainted, faded, and increasingly corrupt. From a Boasean point of view, the authenticity and essence of Native America comes to reside on a bookshelf in a research library rather than Native communities today. Yet I find Christopher Schedler convincing in his assessment that Willa Cather transcends Boas' method to affirm a politics of pluralism. *Death Comes for the Archbishop*, in Schedler's view, demonstrates a sophisticated place in Cather's changing view of anthropology; this novel gives "a dialogic representation of a cultural borderlands peopled by historically situated subjects in specific relations of power."[45] The other writers under consideration here, especially Mary Austin, have similar breakthroughs. Certainly Hieke Schaefer sees Austin's work as progressive: "[Austin] described Native American society and presented place-based Indian cultures as learning models in regional adaptation to her European American readers. She explored the processes of cross-cultural communication and commented on questions of Americanization. Rejecting forced assimilation, she advocated ethnic and cultural diversity."[46] It is worth remembering that these women were progressives of their time and were involved in various activist projects for which they should be applauded. Mabel Dodge Luhan was instrumental in enlisting John Collier in the case of Pueblo land rights. Luhan organized with Alice Corbin and Mary Austin, who wrote for national periodicals on behalf of the cause; while Luhan was not successful in enlisting Cather, she seems to have appreciated the representations of native people in *Death Comes for the Archbishop* as a contribution in the fight.[47]

Perhaps more significantly than their acts of political activism, however, are their acts of the imagination, of creation and affirmation. While I am in agreement with Val Plumwood and others who call for a more rigorous theoretical or philosophical grounding for ecofeminism, I would not wish to utterly discard the importance of a vigorous act of imagination. Taking perhaps the most egregious act of appropriation offered here, Luhan's ingestion of peyote and subsequent vision of a cosmic indigenous holism, it is no difficult matter to dismiss this act of imagination outright. And yet, in that vision of one-ness must be recognized and affirmed the connection between all creation in an ecological totality. If ecofeminism is to offer a counterweight to the Western tradition of human separation from nature and of an empirical science that insists upon demonstrable, repeatable, and measurable relationships in nature, it surely must come in affirming just this sort of creative vision of ecological connection.

For a contemporary indigenous example of ecological theorizing based on oral tradition, I think of Leslie Marmon Silko's *Sacred Water*. In this small book of photographs and text Silko traces her family's attitudes toward snakes and toads as animals associated with rain, linking this reverence to Laguna Pueblo oral traditions regarding the Horned Water Serpent, Ma'sh'ra'tru'ee. The understanding of the natural world in this oral tradition is one of moral responsibility and interconnection. All waters are connected, and human action, including the uranium industry, which contaminates the landscape, contaminates us all.[48] Here I remember Mary Austin's response to the skeptic of pueblo ceremonials calling down rain; Austin asks her skeptical reader to prove that the snake dance does not indeed ensure rain. Rather than supplying evidence that such ceremonies do indeed bring rain, in other words, she asks the skeptic to prove that they do not. This inversion highlights an important split between scientific method and animistic traditions that is still not resolved. In accounts of the impact of uranium mining in Navajo country, we can see a classic sort of intercultural loggerhead: the scientific research shows quantitatively that uranium tailings here do not contaminate groundwater over there. From an indigenous perspective that understands all subterranean water as connected, that understands human action having moral ramifications upon a landscape, scientific findings are unconvincing.[49] And, for those of us concerned with developing an ecocentric consciousness, ultimately we must conclude that whereas the scientific perspective's insistence on measurable results is insufficient, indigenous perspectives highlighting moral responsibility and absolute interconnection are both useful and ultimately accurate.

Notes

1. Carolyn Merchant, *Reinventing Eden: The Fate of Nature in Western Culture* (New York: Rouledge, 2004), 2.

2. Val Plumwood, *Feminism and the Mastery of Nature* (New York: Routledge, 1993), 4.

3. Robert Alter, *Genesis: Translation and Commentary* (New York: Norton, 1996), 13.

4. Marija Gimbutas, *The Language of the Goddess* (New York: HarperCollins, 1989), 121.

5. Gimbutas, 121.

6. Gimbutas, 121.

7. Hamilton A. Tyler, *Pueblo Gods and Myths* (Norman: University of Oklahoma Press, 1964), 234.

8. Ramón Gutiérrez, *When Jesus Came, The Corn Mothers Went Away: Marriage, Sexuality, and Power in New Mexico, 1500-1846* (Stanford, CA: Stanford University Press, 1991), 27-28.

9. Leslie Marmon Silko, *Sacred Water* (Tucson: Flood Plain Press, 1993), 23.

10. Silko, 17.

11. Silko, 17-18.

12. Alice Corbin, *Red Earth: Poems of New Mexico* (Santa Fe: Museum of New Mexico Press, 2003), 52-53.

13. Corbin, 53.

14. Corbin, 77.

15. Corbin, 77-78.

16. Corbin, 71.

17. Corbin, 61.

18. Corbin, 63-65.

19. Corbin, 112.

20. Mary Austin, *The Land of Journey's Ending* (New York: The Century Co., 1924), 269.

21. Austin, 269-70.

22. Austin, 252.

23. Austin, 252.

24. Heike Schaefer, *Mary Austin's Regionalism: Reflections on Gender, Genre and Geography* (Charlottesville: University of Virginia Press, 2004), 149.

25. Austin, 275.

26. Austin, 34.

27. J. W. Fewkes, *The Snake Ceremonials at Walpi* (Ann Arbor: Xerox University Microfilms, 1976), 119.

28. Lois Palken Rudnick, *Mabel Dodge Luhan: New Woman, New Worlds* (Albuquerque: University of New Mexico Press, 1984), 90.

29. Mabel Dodge Luhan, *Edge of the Taos Desert: An Escape to Reality* (Albuquerque: University of New Mexico Press, 1987), 203.

30. Mabel Dodge Luhan, *Taos Winter* (Santa Fe: Las Palomas De Taos, 1983), 125.

31. Luhan, *Taos Winter*, 203.

32. Luhan, *Edge of the Taos Desert*, 318.

33. Luhan, *Edge of the Taos Desert*, 318.

34. Luhan, *Edge of the Taos Desert*, 311.

35. Willa Cather, *Death Comes for the Archbishop* (New York: Vintage Classics, 1990), 295.

36. Cather, 126-27.

37. Cather, 128.

38. Cather, 129.

39. Cather, 129-30.

40. Cather, 132.

41. Charles Lummis, *Some Strange Corners of Our Country: The Wonderland of the Southwest* (Tucson: University of Arizona Press, 1989), 47-48.

42. Cather, 232.

43. Cather, 233.

44. Audrey Goodman, *Translating Southwestern Landscapes: The Making of an Anglo Literary Region* (Tucson: University of Arizona Press, 2002), 165.

45. Goodman, *Translating Southwestern*, 118.

46. Schaefer, *Mary Austin's Regionalism*, 2-3.

47. Rudnick, *Mable Dodge Luhan,*178; 189.

48. Silko, 76.

49. Peter H. Eichstaedt, *If You Poison Us: Uranium and Native Americans* (Santa Fe: Red Crane Books, 1994), 148

3

Littoral Women Writing from the Margins

Susan A. C. Rosen

Carson and Lindbergh - shore visionaries

The coast, where land and water meet, is a type of ecotone, which can be defined as a transition area between two distinct, but adjoining environmental communities; an edge habitat where two or more ecosystems meet. The shore in particular is a specific type of ecotone, a boundary zone, an area with the greatest potential for change or a place that is more sensitive to change, a place that acts as a threshold. So the coast is not just a boundary or an edge, it is a margin that provides a place for the interaction between two or more ecosystems, which results in the ecotone having properties that do not exist in either of the adjacent ecosystems. It is important to consider a definition of the coast for its realistic as well as metaphoric application. What women coastal nature writers discovered as they approached their subject was that the ecotone, or margin, was rich in discovery and change, that every day, the interaction between water and land yielded new observations and required new ways of examination. Historically, women writing about the coast consistently integrated observations of nature with connections to their lower status in society or to their awareness that the coast could be extended, through metaphor, to reflect domestic issues, environmental issues, societal issues. Because it is an environment that naturally blends two such disparate biotic communities, water and land, it presents a strong model for blending multiple theoretical approaches for female nature writers; thus, I believe that the coast naturally gives rise to early ecofeminism.

In 1955, the *New York Time*'s bestseller list included two books about the coast written by women. Anne Morrow Lindbergh's *Gift from the Sea*, the number one bestseller for over a year, was a wildly successful book, especially popular with women readers. Rachel Carson's *The Edge of the Sea* fluctuated between second, third and fourth place on the *Time's* list, always lagging just behind Lindbergh's book. Though the public often confused the two books and their female authors, both texts drew the public's attention to the littoral, to the edges of the country, and, at first glance, brought to the reader a naturalist's observational vision of the shore. In addition, Carson's reputation as a marine zoologist provided readers with an expectation of a scientific text. Despite the public's confusion that these works were similar versions of nature writing, the two books differed dramatically, yet they were both excellent examples of early ecofeminist texts, texts that sought to express the "interrelations among self, societies, and nature."[1] While neither *Gift from the Sea* nor *The Edge of the Sea* are thought to be strong representations of ecofeminism, I do believe that they provide the historical direction for women to look at nature and examine the connections between place, individuals and communities. It is as though the subject itself, the coast, a place where two different ecosystems meet, land and water, provided the impetus for books that would necessarily blend new and different ways of thinking and writing about nature and humanity.

Rachel Carson began pondering the project that would result in *The Edge of the Sea* in 1948. At first she conceived of the book as a field guide that would introduce the nonscientist reader to the scientific terms connected to the shore, but while writing her field guide she discovered that she could not simply list and explain the coast in purely scientific terms because the subject itself presented her with a struggle. In her first public attempt to show her work about the edge of the sea, she maintained her scientific stance and discourse and in 1953 at an AAAS (American Association for the Advancement of Science) meeting, Carson delivered a purely scientific paper entitled "The Edge of the Sea." The paper was well received, but Carson, according to biographer Linda Lear, appeared dissatisfied, and in the spring of 1954, Carson gave a speech on the same subject, the edge of the sea, at the Theta Sigma Phi Matrix Table Dinner in Columbus, Ohio. That evening, however, her lecture took a decidedly personal turn when she declared to the audience of primarily women journalists, "I believe natural beauty has a necessary place in the spiritual development of any individual or any society. I believe that whenever we substitute something man-made and artificial for a natural feature of the earth, we have retarded some part of man's spiritual growth."[2]

For Carson, her departure from standard scientific discourse and practice in her lecture reflected the same path she was taking while writing her field guide. Ultimately, the shore as a subject, as she came to understand her task, demanded she move beyond a strictly observational book to an interpretative one. Carson wanted to consider the factors involved in caring more for the places where we live. She seems to have begun struggling with the question of how we can understand a place: its science but even more so its subtleties, beauty, problems, history, cultures, changes, and politics.

In the preface to *The Edge of the Sea*, Carson warns readers, "To understand the shore, it is not enough to catalogue its life . . . to pick up an empty shell and say 'this is a Murex,' or 'That is an angel wing.'"[3] "Understanding comes only when, standing on a beach we can sense the long rhythms of earth and sea . . . when we can sense with the eye and ear of the mind the surge of life always beating at its shores-blindly, inexorably pressing for a foothold."[4] Carson, in 1955 (pre-dating her most famous work *Silent Spring*), begins to examine an environmental ethic that discusses the reciprocity between humans and nature. She is at the very early stages of recognizing intimacy and responsibility between the human and the natural world, and, in this book, she is also at the very early stages of determining that serious problems between man and nature lurk at the edge of the sea.

In the second chapter, "Patterns of Shore Life," Carson begins to notice some effects of climate change what we now might call global warming,

> [C]urious changes have been taking place, with many animals invading this cold temperate zone from the south and pushing up through Maine and even into Canada. This new distribution is, of course, related to the widespread change of climate that seems to have set in about the beginning of the century and is now well recognized—a general warming-up noticed first in the arctic regions, then in the sub-arctic, and now in the temperate areas of the northern states. With warmer ocean waters north of Cape Cod, not only the adults but the critically important young stages of various southern animals have been able to survive.[5]

Carson goes on to talk about the climate changes resulting in the sea herring becoming scarce in the north Atlantic areas from Maine to New Jersey and the movement into these areas by species usually found to the south such as menhaden, round herring, mantis shrimp, and Whiting. Only a few pages of this chapter are devoted to Carson's observations of specific invading species, the species they replace, and the adverse affect of climate change on the life of the shore. While there is no call to action, a careful reader notices words like "critical" and "survival" in Carson's discourse, and small quiet alarms begin to ring.

Carson is preoccupied with the way the shore brings humans closer to a sense of the past, of what is ancient in the world and at the very same moment, fleeting. So perhaps, this is why she just notes the climate changes rather that asking readers to react. She has not yet made her shift into activist; she is still trying to work as an observer, convinced that the shore itself provides some explanations to her questions about migrating species and survival. Carson also connects the shore and humans through metaphors of dwellings, of homes. In "The Rim of Sand" examining a Georgia sand flat at low tide, she writes,

> I was always aware that I was treading on the thin rooftops of an underground city. Of the inhabitants themselves little or nothing was visible. There were chimneys and stacks and ventilating pipes of underground dwellings, and various passages and runways leading down into darkness. There were little heaps of refuse that had been brought up to the surface as though in an attempt at some sort of civic sanitation.[6]

Here Carson imposes a vision of her own world, one where refuse is hauled out of the house once a week, placed by the curb so that early morning garbage men might come along and dispose of it. She imagines the starfish and ghost shrimp using chimneys or moving through their city along constructed runways. That she reconstructs an image of a human home place to describe the shore is a departure from the scientific discourse of much of the book and belies her need to connect home space with natural space.

Early in the book, Carson comments, "Like the sea itself, the shore fascinates us who return to it, the place of our dim ancestral beginning. In the recurrent rhythms of tides and surf and in the varied life of the tide lines there is the obvious attraction of movement and change and beauty. There is also, I am convinced, a deeper fascination born of inner meaning and significance."[7] While she does not speak of our human role in the changing water temperatures that might lead to the survival of one species over another, she remains convinced that the shore offers an answer path and in "its [the edge of the sea] very pursuit we approach the ultimate mystery of Life itself"[8] Edward Casey in "Body, Self and Landscape" writes, "In effect, there is no place without self; and no self without place."[9] Place constitutes self; shapes identity, and so place is essential to the self. What Carson discovers in *The Edge of the Sea* is that if she looks at the coast through the metaphor of home, and she asks her readers to pay attention to the subtle changes in her home place: the physical, emotional, and ultimately moral, that her work is more satisfying that just writing the original field guide project she was contracted to write. While Carson works through this project from 1948 to 1955, the society at large is going through an interesting advance and retreat in terms of the feminist movement, on the historical surface, a dormant period. However, post WWII, the Rosie's of the time are quietly insisting on staying part of the workforce, young women are earning more college degrees and advanced degrees, and Carson, working in a primarily male dominated field, finds that she must write her scientific field guide using a first person narrative, a commonly used feminist approach, as she tells the reader intimate stories of the coast.

In 1955, *Gift from the Sea*, by Anne Morrow Lindbergh quickly climbed to the top of best-seller lists around the U.S, remaining at the top for an astounding eighty weeks. In its first year of publication, it sold over 300,000 copies.[10] According to her biographer, Susan Hertog, Lindbergh, like Thoreau, wanted to "confirm the lessons of nature in a mechanical age and the divinity of self revelation through meditation. But Anne's solitude, unlike Thoreau's, had a singular purpose-to enrich and consecrate her relationships. Family, Community and State-these were institutions that exalted one's humanity. To live for oneself alone was the stuff of sin"[11] Lindbergh, like Carson, is product of her time, using the metaphors of home and domesticity to examine nature, and Lindberg's work, like Carson's, breaks through traditional gender rhetoric. While many readers and reviewers consider Lindbergh's book philosophy, and most bookstore shelve it in the Women's Studies or Philosophy sections, I believe it is worth considering in the realm of nature writing and early ecofeminism. Lindbergh is a careful, patient and educated observer of nature.

The basic premise of Lindbergh's book, a book that primarily uses the metaphor of the shell to explore one's inner spiritual path, focuses the reader's attention on connections between nature and humanity, with the ultimate emphasis on human. The book includes eight essays, six written around metaphors of shells, which reflect not only Lindbergh's journey inward, but also follow the biological and social life of women. She takes the reader through the stages of leaving home, marriage, middle-age, late-stage marriage after child bearing and rearing, and so on. Lindbergh writes, "The Shell in my hand is deserted. It once housed a whelk, a snail-like creature, and then temporarily, after the death of the first occupant, a little hermit crab, who has run away, leaving his track behind him like a delicate vine on the sand. He ran away, and then left me his shell."[12] For Lindbergh, the discovery of the shell is a point of departure from the physical place where she stands observing the whelk, a point where she can then journey into her interior world. She holds the shell and considers, "I mean to lead a simple life, to choose a simple shell I can carry easily-like a hermit crab. But I do not. I find that my frame of life does not foster simplicity. My husband and five children must make their way in the world. The life I have chosen as wife and mother entrains a whole caravan of complications."[13] Later on in the chapter she exclaims, "What circus acts we women perform every day of our lives"[14] As she considers the demands society has placed on her as a woman of the 1950s she discovers how oppressive the role is and how when left to live according to the natural rhythms of the shore, she finds a new way to live more simply and peacefully. Lindberg comments that these millions of American women are not nurtured by the hectic fragmented lives they lead but are instead being spiritually destroyed by modern demands. Lindbergh's book ultimately leads readers toward finding a balance in the triad of coastal living (nature), societal demands, and women's needs. The notion of balance is crucial to her philosophy and it is, I believe, born out of her observations of coastal balance. The more she walked the shoreline, the more she came to understand the shore as a "place where distinctions slip away; where there is no time, no culture, and no preconceived notion of sexual identity,"[15] a place that found balance between water and land, time and timelessness.

While many have attributed Lindbergh's literary success to her husband's celebrity status, and the media blitz that followed the tragic kidnapping and death of her son, *Gift from the Sea* withstands the test of time primarily due to

Lindbergh's integration of a naturalist's firsthand observation with a discussion of the spiritual growth of the individual as well as the spiritual connection between natural beauty and society. Lindbergh reveals how the sea can give gifts to those who take the time to be contemplative. She writes,

> One learns first of all in beach living the art of shedding; how little one can get along with, not how much. Physical shedding to begin with, which then mysteriously spreads into other fields. Clothes, first. . . . Next, Shelter. . . . Here I live in a bare sea-shell of a cottage. No heat, no telephone, no plumbing to speak of, no hot water. . . . No rugs. . . . find I am shedding hypocrisy in human relationships. . . . I have shed my mask.[16]

She goes on to discuss shedding the need to clean and maintain order, the need for protection and a desire to open the windows—invisible barriers to the natural world. Lindbergh's work ultimately uses place to discuss a better way of living in that place. She seeks to teach her reader about a way to live more simply with nature and within society. Like Carson, what may have begun as a walk along the beach has turned into a book that forces the reader to consider the importance of one's behavior in nature and society.

When searching for the roots of ecofeminism, an interesting array of acknowledged beginnings surface. Some theorists point toward Francoise d'Eaubonne, who introduced the term *eco-feminisme* in her 1974 text *Le feminisme ou la mort* as triggering the ecofeminsim movement. In her 1978 text, *Ecologie-feminisme: revolution ou mutation,* d'Eaubonne solidifies her thesis of the connection between the oppression of women and nature. Other theorists consider Carolyn Merchant's 1980 text, *The Death of Nature: Women, Ecology and the Scientific Revolution* a significant stimulus for contemporary ecofeminism. In this text Merchant clearly argues that the historical patriarchal prerogative to control women and nature when she notes,

> But while the pastoral tradition symbolized nature as a benevolent female, it contained the implication that nature when plowed and cultivated could be used as a commodity and manipulated as a resource. Nature, tames and subdues, could be transform into a garden to provide both material and spiritual food to enhance the comfort and soothe the anxieties of me distraught by the demands of the urban world and the stresses of the marketplace.[17]

According to Charis Thompson, Merchant establishes, "that the domination of women and the domination of nature are structurally linked."[18] Both d'Eaubonne and Merchant hold fast to one dominant notion, that women and nature were oppressed, commodified and ultimately abused by the same dualistic patriarchal system. But later ecofeminism has taken on more breadth. Scholars and activists simply do not agree on the parameters of ecofeminism and when "[b]rowsing the literature we find ecofeminism variously described as a political stance, a-take-it-to-the-streets movement, a feminist spiritual affirmation, an inspirational wellspring for women's activism, a retrieval of womanist earth wisdom, a feminist theory, an applied scholarship, a feminist rebellion within a radical environmentalism, an oppositional positionality, praxis, and a remapping of women's relationship to place and ecology."[19] Ecofeminism is difficult to define, difficult to limit, and its roots are slippery.

What we might say with some confidence is that much of the prominent work of ecofeminism as been done in the past thirty years. Scholars and activists such as Carolyn Merchant, Vandana Shiva, Starhawk, Karen Warren, Greta Gaard, and many others have, since the 1980s, explored the various aspects of ecofeminism in their work and have thus shaped its definition. What interests me are the first whispers of ecofeminism that I hear when reading Rachel Carson's early works or Anne Morrow Lindberg's popular book of place and spirituality, for both of these authors feel compelled by their sense of place to write books that cross disciplinary boundaries and intimately connect these women's philosophies of life to the shore. These texts should not be taken as mere rambles along the ocean coasts. Instead, we can see Rachel Carson allowing herself to identify with the connecting yet juxtaposed environments of sea and land as inspiration for combining her scientific discourse with her humanistic response to nature, a writing tool she would need to create *Silent Spring*. Lindberg, too, while rarely acknowledged by scholars, opened up a discourse community for women to connect their spirituality and societal roles with nature. Thus, Lindberg may have pointed the way for ecofeminist spiritualism, while Carson most certainly pointed the way toward ecofeminist activism.

Ackerman and Buckles—naturalists by profession

Half a century after Carson and Lindbergh published their works drawing the public's attention to the coast, it is possible to see a tradition emerging in women's coastal nature writing. Two contemporary female coastal nature writers worth considering as part of this tradition are Jennifer Ackerman and Mary Parker Buckles. Both of these writers focus their attention on the coast, arm themselves with scientific knowledge, and neither can resist the urge to enter the word pictures they create. Ultimately, Ackerman and Buckles ecofeminist texts rely on an interdisciplinary approach to the subject of the coast weaving together literature, science, sociology, philosophy, history, environmentalism and religion.

Jennifer Ackerman grew up in a world of deciduous woodland landscapes, but in 1998, she moved to the Delaware coast. Initially, she found life at the seashore, as she recounts in her book *Notes from the Shoreline*, disorienting. She felt confused by the winds, disgusted by the odors of the tidal marshes, frustrated by her lack of knowledge about the shore birds and their habits, and yet, slowly, she overcomes her early disdain for the coast as she begins walking along the shore, keeping a journal of her daily observations and seeking guidance in understanding her new environment. Of particular interest is her chapter, "Between Tides" where Ackerman focuses on the stretch of sand between high and low tides known as the littoral, a margin that is home to copepods, nematodes, ostercods, tardigrades, and meiofauna such as rotifers and diatoms. She is fascinated with the complexity and variety of this seemingly invisible micro-community. While most of this chapter follows in the vein of Rachel Carson's initial impulse to write a field guide to explain in scientific terms the creatures of the shore, Ackerman, like Carson and Lindbergh, cannot resist the pull of oppositions and connections. After trogging through the mud flats, she muses, "To Sway outside yourself and dwell in other lives. I think of this ability as a sort of specialized muscle, kept firm only by use. It grows soft from neglect. But the nerve that fires it never flags. . . . That nerve is an ancient, instinctive kinship for wild things, which fires right on down a life."[20] Sounding much like Anne Morrow Lindbergh, Ackerman crosses her observational line into another realm.

Ackerman also shows her indebtedness to Carson and Lindbergh when she ponders the power of the shore on humans. "People move to the littoral like moths to a porch light," she says.[21] Like many before her, she wants to know, "What is the draw of the edge?"[22] She determines, like Carson and Lindbergh that the seashore reveals mysteries that enable humans to connect with unwritten history. "For people like me who measure their land in square feet, not acres, who have lost the rhythm of harvest, the surge and drain of the tides threads the day, gives the place a kind of meter, as in poetry. . . . its briny surf and shifting sand correspond to a memory as deep as any we possess."[23] Hopefully, not to beat the point to death, but it becomes clear when reading Ackerman's prose, that when she writes about the shore she cannot help but reflect on the modern world and its disconnect from history and nature. Her book is filled with the same sorts of subtle requests Carson makes of her readers: know nature, connect to nature, understand how the life you lead has taken you away from the natural, care for nature. However, in Ackerman's late twentieth century case, the damage humans have caused is well documented, and she works hard in this text to promote an alternative to past negative behaviors. She writes,

> I know that one picture of ourselves as agents of death, hurling harpoons at a wounded earth, scurrying toward suicide, making beautiful things disappear and turning the rest to lead is only half of the story. Immense curiosity and filial love of life threaded in our genes is driving us in quite a different direction. Our activity, like our science, gives rise to truths as well as hoaxes. I only hope that we are stumbling, despite ourselves, on an erratic path toward a deeper understanding of nature and a more dignified, honorable relationship with it.[24]

Mary Parker Buckles, author of *Margins: A Naturalist Meets Long Island Sound*, is yet another transplant to the shore. Like Carson, Lindbergh, and Ackerman, she brings her outsider's perspective to her new coastal world, focusing her attention, as the others do on the ecotone of the littoral. Though she divides her book into four major sections: "Land," "Air," "Water," and "Intertidal Zone," these sections are deceiving. In "Land," for example, Buckles writes about the shore and in her other chapters, while she may be looking at the "Air," she is writing about shorebirds: ospreys, cormorants, black-bellied plovers, ruddy turnstones, dunlins. Buckles lets the reader know early in her text that the shore she is exploring, the shore she is beginning to love and understand is a shore abused by humans. She writes,

> This beach and cove, like many others along the sound attracts beer cans and other throwaways that remind me I don't live near wilderness. Juice bottles, and braided ropes, and pink ribbons that wished someone three yards of "Happy Birthday Happy Birthday Happy Birthday," and aquamarine sea glass, and one quart plastic containers printed with the words "Ursa Super Plus SAE 40 Heavy Duty Engine Oil" above the red and white Texaco star are all here.[25]

Buckles reminds me of Pogo, standing at the edge of his swamp and quietly stating, "We have met the enemy and he is us."[26] So she walks her shore and learns like Carson, Lindbergh and Ackerman, and she pays very close attention to the cycles of life. She seeks guides and teachers who will explain what she cannot understand, among them, scientists, birders, photographers and even poets such as Amy Clampitt. Yes, Buckles, like Carson and Lindbergh and Ackerman falls in love with the shore as she learns to see her landscape as sacred but permanently scarred.

What is most important to note, finally, when one reads Buckles, is that Buckles documents the destruction of the coast, its oppression by mankind, as she tries to persuade her readers of the inherent value of saving the severely damaged Long Island Sound and shore. In her "Afterword" Buckles explains that the Sound, post WWII through the 1970s, was the sight of exceptional growth and development and of unchecked environmental abuse. Despite the 1972 Clean Water Act's reach into the Sound, the estuary and the shorelines continue to suffer from high polluting sewage treatment plants, car pollution runoff from black top roads, chemically enhanced lawns, and the many other problems that occur when too many people live in such a fragile environment. She ends her book by asking her readers to consider, "that the way each of us lives, including the water-related habits we acquire and the peace of mind we develop in multiple ways, is brought to bear on the abundant life associated with their body of water [the Long Island Sound]. For just as the Sound is a part of our natural heritage, the very fact that some 8.5 million of us live in her watershed makes us her people."[27] In *Margins: A Naturalist Meets the Long Island Sound*, she has personalized and feminized the damaged estuary while joining a sisterhood of nature writers who have done the same in their efforts to call attention to marginal places.

The literary theorist Mikhail Bahktin once noted that the most creative work of a culture takes place on its margins. Rachel Carson, Anne Morrow Lindbergh,

Jennifer Ackerman, and Mary Parker Buckles and others such as Jan DeBlieu, Gretal Erlich, Sarah Orne Jewett, Nancy Lord, Kathleen Dean Moore, Mary Oliver, May Sarton, and Celia Thaxter occupy both a literary and ecological niche as women nature writers drawn to coasts, drawn to the margins. For these women, the coasts they write about are crucial to their understandings of themselves and to their broader vision of humans and nature. They find it impossible to talk about coasts in purely scientific or philosophical or literary terms, instead, like the landscape they write about, they integrate discourses and disciplines. Carson, Lindbergh, Ackerman and Buckles are place-based writers, but a place cannot express itself until it inspires someone to know the place intimately, to care about the place as though it is home, and then write that place into existence. By critically examining edge spaces where water and land meet, women nature writers raise new variations on critical questions of relationships between nature and culture and of the relationship between women and nature. When looked at as a group of writers rather than individuals who find themselves writing about the shores, it becomes clear that the women naturalists have focused a great deal of their attention to shore issues further exploring constantly shifting margins of women's lives in connection to nature, society, and their inner worlds, that the shore itself has provided a biotic community for ecofeminists to emerge.

Notes

1. Janis Birkeland, "Ecofeminism: Linking Theory and Practice," *Ecofeminism: Women, Animals, Nature,* ed. Greta Gaard, (Philadelphia: Temple University Press, 1993), 18.

2. Linda Lear, *Rachel Carson: Witness for Nature*, (New York: Henry Holt and Company,1997), 259.

3. Rachel Carson, *The Edge of the Sea*, (New York: Signet Books, 1955), xiii.

4. Carson, xii.

5. Carson, 32.

6. Carson, 124.

7. Carson, vii.

8. Carson, 250.

9. Edward Casey, "Body, Self, and Landscape: A Geo-philosophical Inquiry into the Place World," *Textures of Place: Exploring Humanist Geographies*, ed. P. Adams, (Minneapolis: University of Minnesota Press, 2001), 406.

10. Susan Hertog, *Ann Morrow Lindbergh: Her Life,* (New York: Doubleday, 1999), 433–34.

11. Hertog, 434.

12. Anne Morrow Lindbergh, *Gift from the Sea,* (New York: Pantheon Books, 1955, 1997), 21.

13. Lindbergh, 25.

14. Lindbergh, 25.

15. Hertog, 428.

16. Lindbergh, 30–31.

17. Carolyn Merchant, *The Death of Nature: Women, Ecology and the Scientific Revolution*, (San Francisco: Harper & Row Publishers, 1983), 8–9.

18. Charis Thompson, "Back to Nature? Resurrecting Ecofeminism After Poststructuralist and Third-wave Feminisms," *Isis* 97.3 (Sept 2006): 505–13.

19. Joni Seager, "Rachel Carson Died of Breast Cancer: the Coming of Age of Feminist Environmentalism," *Signs* 28.3 (Spring 2003): 945–74.

20. Jennifer Ackerman, *Notes From the Shore*, (New York: Penguin Books, 1995), 71.

21. Ackerman, 30.

22. Ackerman, 30.

23. Ackerman, 31.

24. Ackerman, 169

25. Mary Parker Buckles, *A Naturalist Meets the Long Island Sound,* (New York: Farrar, Strauss and Giroux, 1997), 19–20.

26. Walt Kelly, *Pogo: We Have Met the Enemy and He is Us*, (New York: Simon Schuster, 1972), cover.

27. Buckles, 282–83.

4

Multifaceted Dialogues: Toward an Environmental Ethic of Care

Barbara J. Cook

Over the last few decades, writers, philosophers, naturalists, activists, and other lovers of the outdoors have pointed to the necessity for a change in the way we view and think about the natural world. This change has been difficult to initiate, even harder to accomplish on a large scale. The difficulty in this challenge is that the tradition of scientific thinking distances us from nature. The reasoned thinking that grew out of the Enlightenment places nature as other, an entity to be controlled, utilized, objectified, oppressed. Feminists, especially ecofeminists, have pointed to the oppression of the natural world as indicative of and linked to the oppression of others—women, people of color, people of differing gender and sexual orientation, people with disabilities. Feminist theory names the "framework that authorizes these forms of oppression as patriarchy, an ideology whose fundamental self/other distinction is based on a sense of self that is separate, atomistic."[1] This divide is reflected by many women who incorporate nature into their writing and they often struggle to bridge the dualism of self/other in their own work.

Activist and scholar Greta Gaard points to studies that show men and women commonly view the self differently—men have a sense of self as separate while women have a sense of an interconnected self.[2] These different understandings of self have been found to create differing ethical systems. A self that operates on the basis of an ethic of rights or justice is founded on a separate sense of self while an interconnected sense of self leads to making "moral decisions on the basis of an ethic of responsibility of care."[3] Karen Warren, Marti Kheel, and other feminist scholars see this as a feminist moral ethic that is "a natural outgrowth of how one views the self, including one's relation to the rest of the world."[4] Nature writers have long attempted to place the natural world in dialogue with human experience and the human spirit. These have often incorporated the writers solitary, sometimes isolated experiences. I believe that nature writer and philosopher Kathleen Dean Moore creates a more interconnected reading of nature than many in the past have provided. In the feminist tradition of multiple voices, Moore presents a tapestry of voices that includes not only her voice and that of the natural world but sets up a dialogue that engages our families, our relationships, our daily lives.

The dialogue that Moore creates in her work leads to an ethic of care that clearly reflects recent feminist thinking on moral ethics. In this essay I argue that in her body of work, Kathleen Dean Moore adroitly leads us to an understanding of this ethic of care. In her third collection of essays, she delineates her own thoughts on caring for the natural world as a necessary outgrowth of ethics and morality; but, in her early works she has already begun to draw us into that interconnected sense of self which makes the ecofeminist ethical approach obtainable.

In Moore's first collection of essays, *Riverwalking: Reflections on Moving Water*, she takes us traveling through the West, often with her family, as she rafts down rapids, camps in the desert, hikes over dunes, walks in and beside rivers. All along the way, she shares with us her observations about love, loss, aging, motherhood, and happiness. Moore blends experience and observation, with knowledge and science and with memory and personal life. In the preface to this collection, Moore writes:

> I have come to believe that all essays walk in rivers. Essays ask the philosophical question that flows through time—How shall I live my life? The answers drift together through countless converging streams, where they move softly below the reflective surface of the natural world and mix in the deep and quiet places of the mind. This is where an essayist must walk stirring up the mud.[5]

She asks, "How should I live my life?" and for her, the answers are found moving below the surface of the natural world and mixed in mud and quiet places of the mind. The very question as to how to exist is interconnected—mind and mud.

In the first essay, "The Williamette," Moore interweaves a family camping trip the weekend before her daughter leaves for Greece and biographical details of her parents and grandparents, stressing a sense of home; memories of her own home and her first apartment after she was married, and her childhood home in Cleveland. She also touches on a philosophical discussion of going home and homing instincts in garter snakes with brief references to bees. Her conclusion connects how wasps find their holes by returning to a remembered location with her own realization of the ways in which home is given meaning by a person.

Holdfast: At Home in the Natural World, her second collection, begins with an epigraph, a definition from Rachel Carson's writing: "**Holdfast**: A rootlike structure, as of algae and other simple plants, for attachment to the substrate."[6]

Her "Prologue" meditates on the bullwhip kelp along the Oregon coast which is held in place by a holdfast and asks what is it that holds us together in our times of many separations—"the comings and goings at the turning of the century, the airport embraces, the X-ray rooms, loneliness, notes left by the phone."[7] She proposes that human beings forget we are part of the natural world and are only sometimes reminded by a "sadness we can't explain and a longing for a place that feels like home."[8] In introducing this collection, Moore writes: "Sitting on a boulder whitewashed by western gulls, watching the sliding surf, I resolve to study holdfasts. What will we cling to, in the confusion of the tides? What structures of connection will hold us in place: How will we find an attachment to the natural world that makes us feel safe and fully alive, here, at the edge of water?"[9]

Environmental writers argue that ecological wisdom requires each of us to know our local ecology intimately. Even though Moore is intimately interconnected to the natural world, she questions the necessity for extensive knowledge of a local landscape as the only way to remain connected to nature. She notes that you can put down roots by staying in one place but she also observes that each winter the holdfast of mature kelp plants sheds "thousands of spores that drift off in the currents, gradually settling on the ocean floor. Wherever a spore lands—on a cobble or a pile of broken shells or on bedrock—it grows strong green fingers that hold on tight, while the plant grows quickly toward the light."[10]

Subtlety, she suggests a way for her daughter Erin to feel at home no matter where she is. "It's a kind of rootedness that has to do with noticing, with caring, with remembering, with embracing, with rejoicing in the breadth of the horizon and taking comfort in the familiar smell of rain. In the sliding shifting world my daughter lives in, this may be the closest thing to bedrock."[11]

In my own "sliding shifting" world of academia these words bring me comfort. I have always been drawn to Moore's writing and I am beginning to understand that it is the way she draws her human/nature connections that keeps me returning to her work. The week I reread portions of *Holdfast,* I also said goodbye to my daughter at the Pittsburgh airport as she flew off to Los Angeles, where she will soon leave for a training period in Chicago for her new job, a job that will relocate her somewhere in the United States.[12] I know that we will both have a holdfast to anchor ourselves and our relationship.

In her work, Moore links the love of family with the love of place and they are both encompassed in what she calls an "ecology . . . of caring."[13] In her third book, *Pine Island Paradox: Making Connections in a Disconnected World,* she proposes an environmental ethic of care. To develop this philosophy Moore, fuses Aldo Leopold's land ethic and feminist Nel Noddings's ethics of care. Although Moore, makes this connection herself, this fusion would seem problematic as many feminist scholars have criticized Leopold's land ethic as an ethic of restraint of aggression rather than an ethics of nurturing or caring.

Aldo Leopold points out that, philosophically, an ethic "is a differentiation of social from anti-social conduct."[14] Leopold notes that throughout civilization the notion of ethical behavior has been extended to include women, slaves, and others originally not included by the Greek philosophers. He writes that ethics can be considered from both a philosophical view and an ecological view. Ecologically, an ethic "is a limitation on freedom of action in the struggle for existence."[15] Leopold argues that all ethics rest upon the single premise that "the individual is a member of a community of interdependent parts. . . . The land ethic simply enlarges the boundaries of the community to include soils, waters, plants, and animals, or collectively: the land."[16] He argues that this change in ethics changes the role of the human from one of "conqueror of the land-community to plain member and citizen of it."[17] It is Leopold's notion of "limitation on freedom of action," quoted above that points to the roots of the criticism. Kheel argues that for Leopold, ethics "enters into the picture as the need to curb, *not eliminate*" the aggressive drive that is the heart of the human experience. Kheel quotes his view of hunting:

> Some can live without the opportunity for the exercise and control of the hunting instinct, just as I suppose some can live without work, play, love, business or other vital adventure. But in these days we regard deprivation as unsocial. Opportunity for the exercise of all the normal instincts has come to be regarded more and more as an inalienable right."[18]

Note: Leopold does not see killing the animals as the problem but rather the excessive killing of animals which ruins opportunities for other hunters to kill. Even though Leopold advocates a change in the way we view the natural world, it must come through an internal change as well as an understanding of the human connection to that world. However, Leopold's ethic does seem to be rooted in an ethics based on a separation or divide of self/nature which is out of step with the ethics of caring that Moore proposes and illustrates in her work. The work of Nel Noddings seems more appropriate.

Noddings, a feminist who has written prolifically about the importance of caring in education, emphasizes the importance of personal relationships as the foundation for ethical conduct. Her philosophical argument asserts that the basis for moral action is caring and the memory of being cared for. She writes: "Ethical caring's great contribution is to guide action long enough for natural caring to be restored and for people once again to interact with mutual and spontaneous regard."[19] Noddings proposes a realignment of education to encourage and reward not just rationality and trained intelligence, but also enhanced sensitivity in moral matters. I see Nodding's relationships as an ecofeminist interconnectedness of self, others, nature.

Moore writes that humans are born into relationships with each other and with the land. We naturally care as Noddings points out in her work. The question then becomes for me, how do we extend recognition of that caring to the land, to the natural world, to what Leopold calls the biotic community? Moore's work shows us a possible pathway.

This ethic of care that Moore and Noddings write about is one of the most important twentieth century contributions to moral theory.[20] Moore calls for an extension of moral theory—"call it an ecological 'ethic of care,' call it a 'moral ecology.' It's an ethic built on caring for people *and* caring for places, and on the intricate and beautiful ways that love for places and love for people nurture each other and sustain us all."[21] Moore's previous collections of essays provide ample examples of the ways in which love for people and love for places are connected and enrich each other. However, in *The Pine Island Paradox*, she makes those links crystal clear in ways that can lead to the internal changes that must be made in order to develop an ethic of care, a moral ecology.

Moore begins by gauging three "separations drawn onto the worldviews of the Western World": the claim of a separation between human beings and nature, "the illusion that our individual well-being can be disconnected from the well-being of the biological and social systems that sustain us," and the separation of the sacred from the mundane. [22] She draws on a geographical analogy, ground-truth which links the abstract patterns of maps and aerial photographs to the actuality of the ground. *Pine Island Paradox* is, for Moore, the "ground-truthing of environmental ethics."[23] One of the early questions she asks is what it means to love a place. This meditation is wrapped in the story of one of the family trips to Pine Island that coincides with her thirty-second wedding anniversary. She seeks to understand the complicated ways that love for people and love for places are intertwined. She begins with a list for each love—place and people. However, they turn out to be the same. Love for people and love for place are evidenced by wanting to be physically near; to want to know the story, the moods of the person/landscape; to rejoice in it; to fear its loss and to be transformed in its presence. There is a sense of wanting to be joined with it, lost in it, "to want the best for it. . . . Desperately." Finally, she writes, "Number ten,. . To love a person or a place is to accept moral responsibility for its well-being." [24]

This direct linking of the meanings of love for a person and love for a place leaves no room to doubt humanity's responsibility for caring for our ecological systems. Although many nature writers interact with landscapes in seeming isolation, Moore offers a relationship to the land that includes the ones we love. Writers like Edward Abbey and Henry David Thoreau, from all accounts, carefully edited out personal relationships in their works. Moore points out that the philosophers of the Enlightenment, such as René Descartes, mapped out "a miserable, lonely world for us to live in."[25] Moore's linkage of place and loved ones doesn't allow the reader to separate our moral responsibilities to each. She presents a complicated and multilayered portrait of human kinship with the natural world. She makes four points. Humans and the natural world share kinship of common substance, kinship of common origins, kinship of interdependence, and kinship of common fate.[26] Any alteration, any degradation of either ultimately affects the other.

In addition to the humility that Aldo Leopold calls for in caring for the land, Moore points to the need for "ecological literacy, a basic understanding of how the world works" and the need for compassion and moral imagination—the "difficult art of love."[27] But she continues the dialogue as she prepares to return home. For instance, when she prepares to bring a group of students "down the mountain" to the city, she questions how we can bring the values of wildness down with us—in other words, how do we find the moral equivalent of wildness in nearby places? Or, as she contemplates, "maybe this is the question: How can we live *as if we were* in the wilderness, with that same respect and care for what is beautiful and beyond?"[28] Living as if we were in the wilderness could mean much more attention given to our cities, our day to day places. As Moore points out, our moral responsibility should not be different in different places, it doesn't make sense. How many of us have passed signs indicating that we are entering or leaving a ecological watershed area that is miles away, sometimes hundreds of miles away? These signs are reminders that actions often have consequences far away from where they take place. Moore's essays remind constantly of the interconnectedness of our world. she writes:

> Between the wilderness and the town, we would drive through a series of ecological and political landscapes—from the primeval forests, through clear-cuts and tree farms as patchy and tufted as if a child had taken electric clippers to the back of a dog, on through the laser-leveled agricultural fields, to the neighborhoods. On the same journey, we would pass through a set of equally distinct moral landscapes. We would begin in patches of wilderness ethic, where people feel a strong obligation to do no harm, and were hikers enter the land with respect and rejoicing. At the end of the journey are hedge-bordered home places, where people care for the land as if it were a child, tending to its needs, making it beautiful and healthy. But in between is a wide, bewildering swath of moral no-man's-land, where the land is a commodity and people are careless of it, or disdainful, and use it for their own short-term self-interest."[29]

If we seek to take our wildness values home with us, she asks, why don't we also take our moral responsibility to take care of the land wherever we find it? She further questions, what is the necessary education or process of moral development that fosters a person's growth of the moral synapses, "the strong sense that the world-as-it-is asks something of them."[30]

Moore extends this notion of valuing nearby places, in the essay, "Where Should I Live and What Should I Live For?" At one point, she reveals her dream to live in a small cedar house in the wildness because, "Nature writers ever since Thoreau have moved to the woods, deliberately, to learn what it has to teach." [31] As she questions this notion, she acknowledges the possibility that Thoreau "may have set sort of a bad example when he moved to the woods to live deliberately."[32] There is something in this movement toward the wildness, that leaves the impression you can leave destruction behind and writing about nature "out there," makes it harder to remember the nature nearby.[33] Moore, incorporates a story of two thieving blue jays, certainly city birds, into this meditation making the urban/wildness link for us.

She further connects the mundane, everyday world that we live in to the wildness in the final section of the book as she links the mundane to the sacred. She sees the boundary between the ordinary and extraordinary as blurred. The everyday is irreplaceable, essential, beyond human understanding. "The English word for this combination of qualities is "sacred."[34] The intertwining of the mundane and the sacred results in an understanding of the world that encourages awe and, ultimately, gratitude. And, it is gratitude that completes the circle. Moore answers her question, "is gratitude a moral obligation? . . . To be grateful is to live a life that honors the gift."[35] The gift includes the natural world.

The multifaceted dialogues that surface in the essays of Kathleen Dean Moore point to a deeper understanding of the human/nature relationship. For Moore, her philosophical dialogues are critical to her own understanding of what it means to live in this world in such a way that reflects the moral responsibility each of us share and must learn to recognize. Although she, like many nature writers, writes a great deal about the wildness of the mountains, rivers, deserts, and oceans, her closing essays in *Pine Island Paradox* join the dialogue with nature writers and eco-critics who are writing about nature in urban spaces and built environments. She too, argues that urban spaces matter also. Urban, rural, wilderness, these spaces are all connected as is humanity to those spaces. Moore's philosophical musings can lead us to the environmental ethic of care that she proposes—a natural sense of caring for ourselves, our families, and our natural world.

Notes

1. Greta Gaard, ed., *Ecofeminism: Women, Animals, Nature* (Philadelphia: Temple University Press, 1993), 2.

2. Gaard draws on studies by Nancy Chodorow, *The Reproduction of Mothering: Psychoanalysis and the Sociology of Gender* (Berkeley: University of California Press, 1978); Carol Gilligan, *In a Different Voice: Psychological Theory and Women's Development* (Cambridge: Harvard University Press, 1982); Carol Gilligan, Janie Ward, Jill McLean Taylor, and Betty Bardige, eds., *Mapping the Moral Domain* (Cambridge: Harvard University Press, 1988); and Seyla Benhabib, "The Generalized and the Concrete Other: The Kohlberg-Gilligan Controversery and Feminist Theory," in *Feminism as Critique: On the Politics of Gender*, eds. Seyla Benhabib and Drucilla Cornell (Minneapolis: University of Minnesota Press, 1987), 77–95.

3. Gaard, 2.

4. Marti Kheel, "From Heroic to Holistic Ethics," *Ecofeminism: Women, Animals, Nature,* ed. Greta Gaard (Philadelphia: Temple University Press, 1993), 244.

5. Kathleen Dean Moore, *Riverwalking: Reflections on Moving Water* (New York: Harcourt Brace & Company, 1995), xiii.

6. Kathleen Dean Moore, *Holdfast: At Home in the Natural World* (New York: Lyons Press, 1999), xi.

7. Moore, 13.

8. Moore, 14.

9. Moore, 14.

10. Moore, 15.

11. Moore, 15.

12. My daughter was eventually transferred to Miami—a continent away from Los Angeles but at least we are now in same time zone.

13. Moore, 34.

14. Aldo Leopold, *The Sand County Almanac* (New York: Ballantine Books, 1949, 1970), 238.

15. Leopold, 238.

16. Leopold, 239.

17. Leopold, 240.

18. Quoted by Kheel, 252 from Leopold, 262.

19. Nel Noddings and Paul J. Shore. *Awakening the Inner Eye: Intuition in Education*, (Troy, NY: Educator's International Press, 1998).

20. Kathleen Dean Moore, *The Pine Island Paradox: Making Connections in a Disconnected World*.(Minneapolis: Milkweed Press. 2004), 62.

21. Moore, *Holdfast*, 65.

22. Moore, *Pine Island*, 7.

23. Moore, 8.

24. Moore, 35–36.

25. Moore, 53.

26. Moore, 55–56.

27. Moore, 89.

28. Moore, 96.

29. Moore, 100–101.

30. Moore, 114.

31. Moore 131.

32. Moore, 134.

33. Moore, 135.

34. Moore, 180.

35. Moore, 232.

5

Wild Women: Literary Explorations of American Landscapes

Sarah E. McFarland

Traditional American nature writing has been burdened by a discriminatory history, influenced by wilderness exploration and scientific study that excluded women. In canonical American nature writing by folks like Ralph Waldo Emerson, Henry David Thoreau, John Muir, John Burroughs, Aldo Leopold, Ed Abbey, and Barry Lopez, the male narrator demonstrates the manly pursuit of wilderness travel, and nature, the object of their pursuit, is often metaphorically feminine.[1] According to William Cronon, the very notion of "wilderness" depends on a gendered frontier nostalgia: "in the wilderness, a man could be a real man, the rugged individual he was meant to be before civilization sapped his energy and threatened his masculinity."[2] This virile, heroic figure then constructs the landscape using feminine metaphors, further restricting its access by women. As Annette Kolodny argues, "the psychosexual dynamic of a virginal paradise meant . . . that real flesh-and-blood women—at least metaphorically—were dispossessed of paradise."[3] The exclusion of women from nature writing is not a problem only because it disguises the fact that the very concept of wilderness is a male construct, but also because it leaves careful readers with the impression that nature is no place for women.

These American cultural and narrative histories continue to have a significant influence on recent nature writing. The typical construction of nature writing today imagines the first person narrator as a questing hero who abandons the city to create a new, more humble relationship with the natural environment and its inhabitants, in hopes that readers will gain interest in environmental preservation and an awareness of the effects of its degradation and destruction.[4] However, despite their best efforts to create an environmentally sound perspective, writers who unquestioningly accept a gendered vision of nature undermine their projects. How do women authors work to change these preconceived notions about landscape, women, animals, and nature exploration? I argue here that works by Susan Zwinger and Terry Tempest Williams challenge traditional stereotypes about women and nature in acts that powerfully resist the erasure of women from wilderness and turn the historically negative equation of women with nature and animals into a positive experience.

In *The Last Wild Edge: One Woman's Journey from the Arctic Circle to the Olympic Rain Forest*, Susan Zwinger says that she "does not want to write another treatise about the planetary giants, the sexy megafauna at the top of the food chain."[5] Her reasoning goes beyond the fact that most nature writers focus on the charismatic megafauna; she says: "To know the landscape intimately and not just pass through, each one of us must develop the vibrissae of a vole, the nose of a fox, the ears of an owl, the chemical-sensing mycelia of a truffle, the echolocation of a bat, the directional sense of an arctic tern, and the eyes of a bald eagle."[6] In other words, humans must be willing to change their sensory relationship with the land in order to better understand its multifaceted ways, a process that begins in part by recognizing that wilderness is more than the "sexy megafauna" that happen to live there. By changing perspectives in this way, Zwinger aims to "discover the world in a centimeter of lichen and the circumference of a mountain."[7] She happens upon some sexy megafauna as well, when she looks up from the ground.

Central to Zwinger's re-envisioning of human relationships with nature—and, I argue, her subversion of traditional, masculine nature writing themes—are her efforts to recognize the agency of the world around her and the resultant blurring of authorial position and perspective, and her efforts to create a playful undoing of traditional (and often stereotypical) metaphors for animals and women. In her earlier book, *Stalking the Ice Dragon: An Alaskan Journey*, she challenges the myth of a womanless wilderness by literally and literarily inhabiting so-called "wild" space and writing back to the men who preceded her there, striving to redefine how women and animals are perceived in wilderness and conceived in literature. Her descriptions of the powerful and intelligent female humans and animals she encounters are one aspect of this effort—as is, obviously, her own presence in the Alaskan wilderness. Refusing to embody the trope of the solo explorer claiming the untouched wilderness for his own, Zwinger introduces us to the many people she meets and who share her experience. Her choice to humbly interact with the landscapes, people, and other animals around her is rooted in her belief that "everything is a fabric, a whole, a world in which all (from microorganism to president) are entangled irrevocably in each other's oxygen tubes. One big Gordian knot."[8]

Zwinger defines the space in which she travels as "wild" based on the scarcity of humans and the abundance of other animals, like many other nature writers do. It is because of the "uncounted caribou, moose, grizzly and black bear, wolves, beavers, and hoary marmots [that] live unbothered [there]"[9] that Alaska is wild. However, she avoids obliterating the actual animals from her narrative by recognizing the singularity of each individual and by making efforts to recognize the subjectivity of other beings. When she encounters a female moose, for example, she meets her as an equal being. Zwinger says: "I have driven up a sharp rise. At the top I meet, nose-to-nose, a moose. She is a tall bag of bones with loose gray skin draped over a Tinker Toy frame. She appears four times as large as the truck. She looks up calmly, only slightly perturbed at the noise, so I cut the engine and watch her cumbersome magnificence."[10]

Zwinger describes an interaction between two beings on equal ground: each is capable of examining the other. She further articulates the moose's capabilities in the unforgiving landscape:

> Her eyes are dark and gentle, her whole countenance that of a lugubrious wisdom left over from an ice age. She is well built for the harshest of winters, her massive body conserving heat and storing huge amounts of energy. . . . [S]he is capable of great power. I remember photographs of one of her kind, hackles raised, head down, charging a full-grown male grizzly.[11]

The immense power of this huge vegetarian is favorably compared to that of one of the "sexy megafauna"—a male grizzly. Thus, Zwinger implies the dangerousness of the moose species without allowing a simple image of female loveliness—those dark and gentle eyes—to be her most memorable feature. Readers gain a compelling sense of the female moose as a powerful agent in a harsh world, as opposed to a Disneyfied and feminized gentle vegetarian.

It is obvious that issues of gender and subjectivity are quite consciously at the forefront of Zwinger's written accounts of her experiences. Her understanding of both the history of exploratory ventures and the implications of working within such a gendered tradition is clear from her efforts to specify her own stereotypes of gender. For example, she says:

> The first night there is a sense of abandonment and loneliness I had not expected, perhaps based on some gender expectations I have of myself. Historically, it is theman who has left behind wife, children, the court, his kingdom, his queen, his lover to venture forth to the unknown. His essence has always been to expand knowledge, to conquer, to claim new lands, to grow spiritually, to haul back earthly goods—mostly to haul back earthly goods.[12]

Unlike those male explorers, her purpose is to change the way she perceives things—literally—and thus to change her readers' perspectives about women, nature, and animals. She says, "How peculiar is the eye: at first it sees nothing, then a little, and then a proliferation of forms" in a land "so surreal that the mind cannot surround it;"[13] she articulates the animalness of her humanness in passages that describe how her senses change and adapt:

> I am aware of a distinct difference in myself. My senses have changed profoundly in just one month of being alone. At first I am aware of it in eyesight, which has become keen, aware of slight movement. I am seeing far distances without the binoculars. Yet, physically, I see no better. I discern subtle patterns against pattern: a marmot no longer appears to be a rock.
>
> The sense of smell is acute, even though my own body smells more and more like a wild animal. I smell for animals, for water, for fresh plants. . . . And hearing, never very acute for me, awakens with the slightest rustle. A sense of air pressure allows me to know what the weather will do without looking up. . . . As a myriad of unusual minerals in berries and mushrooms enters my tongue, the sense of taste is heightened.
>
> The world has become vividly alive.[14]

Thus, she further undoes the gendered traditions of exploration as seen in American nature writing, because, as she states in *The Last Wild Edge*, she needs courage as well as "legs, knees, and a hand lens" to change perspectives[15]—the courage to enter a literature long dominated by male viewpoints and a willingness to recognize her animalness.

However, there are other ways women have been equated with animals, and Zwinger recognizes the tradition of associating "female" with "animal"—an equation intended to denigrate women. She describes being objectified under that gaze in those terms but cleverly complicates any reading of the associations she makes. She writes, for example, in *Stalking the Ice Dragon*:

> Woman-Travels-Alone up here is a nonsequitur. When I enter a restaurant early in the morning, men gawk at me like deformed game. As in Mexico, I do not look into eyes. They are speaking passionately about something when I walk in, but forks pause in midstroke, mouths remain open, and only slowly is the silence again broken. I walk through their cat's cradle of stares, a cat through a sprinkler system.[16]

While it seems that here Zwinger articulates the sense of being both female and animal under the male gaze of the restaurant patrons, this is only partly true. On the one hand, the men are participating in a kind of "game" that is deformed—a grotesque version of gendered behavior. On the other, however, are more complicated equations of humans and other animals that do not fall along traditional gendered lines. The first equation is ambiguous: "Men gawk at me like deformed game" can mean either that the men gawk like deformed game would gawk, or that the men gawk like they would while watching deformed game. As "game" is both singular and plural, it can refer to either the singular "me" or the plural "men." The second equation of humans to other animals is also complex. In cat's cradle, two people twist and wind a looped string around their hands and pass it back and forth. Zwinger's analogy expresses a sense of being trapped in stares in the same way that cat's cradle players are trapped in the looped string. More than that, however, "their cat's cradle" animalizes the men's part of the interaction—using the word "cat"—just as Zwinger animalizes her own part, "a cat through a sprinkler system," recognizing the sense of insecurity a cat might feel being sprayed with water.

By creating these complicated syntactical ambiguities, Zwinger controls the otherwise derogatory connection society frequently imposes when equating femininity with animality. As Josephine Donovan argues, "The anomalous and the powerless include women and animals, both of whose subjectivities and realities are erased or converted into manipulatable objects—'the material of subjugation'—at the mercy of the rationalist manipulator, whose self-worth is established by the fact that he subdues his environment."[17] Zwinger takes the subduing force—here the male gaze of the restaurant patrons—and disempowers it by opening the equation with other animals to include those men, too.

This is a compelling move, because as Carol Adams indicates, "The traditional feminist response to the equation of femaleness with animalness has been to break that association," not to make it universal.[18] The Western tradition of symbolically aligning the natural with the feminine and the subsequent argument that both need to be controlled and domesticated is something most feminists want to avoid repeating. For example, Kate Soper argues that we need to avoid linguistically "reproduc[ing] the woman-nature equivalence that has served as legitimation for the domestication of women and their relegation to maternal and nurturing functions."[19] Louise Westling proposes that "concerted efforts must be made to shape new metaphors for the land that are neuter and nonanthropomorphic,"[20] suggesting that women as well as men should cease the destructive tradition of equating the feminine with the natural. Instead of a simple comparison, however, I find that Zwinger's performance in this passage goes beyond the traditional equation of female with animal or natural in ways that are worth considering. She embodies the animal perspective as she recognizes the animality of the other humans so as to draw attention to those equations and ultimately break the binary down.

Zwinger further broadens the way we consider things when she redefines the ways animals are conceived in literature. A good example occurs in Zwinger's treatment of one of the most idealized animals in Alaska: grizzly bears. Often described in masculine terms because they are at the top of the food chain, bears are one of the many charismatic megafauna favored by nature writers. As Lynda Birke argues, "[Western ideology] has contributed to notions of different kinds of animals that relate to gender or social class; fierce beasts acquire the demeanour of virile masculinity, purring puss-cats are the epitome of cuddly femininity."[21] But Zwinger is careful to maintain a neutral vocabulary as she describes her experience. Her encounter with a bear is one in which she expresses a sense of awe at what she sees, not at some imposed notion of its masculinity, and readers can feel the scene unfold:

> Exhausted after the tundra haul, I shall never move again. Until, against the dark gray stone wall, white dots are moving! . . . One-half-mile along a precarious edge I move until they develop legs. Sheep legs! A little closer and they have heads and are grazing pastorally on a green shoulder of mountain. One up on the ridge has run down and appears to be "playing" frantically with the others, butting them into a knot. How odd: this play among adults who should conserve precious energy for winter.[22]

We experience her discovery of the dots that become sheep and her confusion at their strange behavior here. As readers, we are also excited to figure out what is going on—as if we were there, experiencing it alongside her. She continues:

> Closer. Look again. Can't believe my eyes: a dark figure lumbers after them. A wolf? No, too large.
>
> Bear! Huge white slash down its side and a muscular hump on its back. Grizzly! My hands shake.
>
> Bear! My circulation stops, adrenaline zings out to my fingertips and toes. Not out of fear, but out of respect. The while slash and the muscular hump chant grizzly. The magnificent beast at the top of the food chain.[23]

This bear has no gender; it is magnificent and respected simply because it is a grizzly—and this is significant because it would be easy to use gendered stereotypes to portray the bear and sheep because of the western cultural assumptions we hold about sheep as flock-oriented feminine food animals and bears as tough independent masculine ones. As Barney Nelson says, "Wild males are imagined as big, strong leaders with the skills to live off the land, their lives free, violent, and unencumbered by such boring domestic responsibilities as tending children."[24] Zwinger does not project these kinds of gendered stereotypes onto what she sees: she simply expresses her reaction to discovering the cause of the sheep's distress and her excitement at seeing a bear.

While Zwinger is not personally afraid to discover a bear nearby, she does feel empathy for the sheep, further broadening our understanding of the situation. She writes: "I try to imagine how frightened those four must feel: the loss of precious feeding ground and time; to stand now on a steep scree, balancing, watching, always wary."[25] By recognizing the perspective of the sheep and identifying with their struggle for survival amidst her own confusion, Zwinger helps broaden our understanding of the "reality" of the scene. No one position is a dominant one. Donna Haraway describes such a change in the study of nature when she discusses the formation of a new kind of scientist:

> Science becomes the myth not of what escapes human agency and responsibility in a realm above the fray, but rather of accountability and responsibility for translations and solidarities linking the cacophonous visions and visionary voices that characterize the knowledges of the subjugated. A splitting of senses, a confusion of voice and sight, rather than clear and distinct ideas, becomes the metaphor for the ground of the rational.[26]

Zwinger refuses to occupy the place of the invisible scientist-observer here by articulating her human confusion and misunderstanding and expresses the position of another being as best she can imagine it. No single position is defined exclusively; rather, both are located with clarity.

Furthermore, Zwinger forces her readers to experience her human-as-bodily-animal confusion and physiological reaction to recognizing a grizzly by not applying cultural or scientific conclusions onto the scene. This move is precisely opposite from the turn toward more traditional scientific ways of seeing in which the scientist-observer sees all from a bodiless distance that Haraway describes above. Zwinger is an author who expresses, to use the words of Margaret Homans, what she "sees before she reads" an experience, refusing "to obliterate the image in favor of meaning."[27] In other words, Zwinger offers so many perspectives that she does not reinforce the hierarchies of power that insist on a single conclusion about nature.

As the passage progresses, Zwinger further undoes typical gender assumptions as she imagines the perspectives of the sheep and bear. As quoted previously, she feels pity for the sheep and the energy they waste running from the bear, saying "I try to imagine how frightened those four must feel."[28] Even though the awe she expresses earlier in the passage is not the result of the bear's perceived masculine traits, when she does assign gender she modifies the usual roles. She finally gives the bear a gender—male—but goes a step further, imagining his perspective by *becoming* him:

> I think as the hunter, too, crawling into his bear skin and wandering in his bear mind and bear body, crossing steep scree, the pads of my feet sore on the volcanic stone. There is nausea in the pit of my stomach; muscles ache with it. . . . Just one fat-sheathed sheep could make all the difference. . . . I hurdle through tundra in the dusk, seeing in my brain's eye the blood-twitching red meat, the delicious fat hanging in drapes from the inside of the skin. I feel my powerful jaws crushing down on the skull with delight, the brain squirting out, protein rich caviar, that greasy thick wool in my mouth.[29]

Zwinger imagines herself and the male bear as one, successfully killing the sheep that might make the difference between survival or death in the long hungry winter. She places herself in the position we would normally consider most powerful (the masculine hunter), instead of the position traditionally considered weak (the feminine hunted). She further complicates that very notion of superiority by articulating the severity of the hunger she—as a bear—might feel.

Lynda Birke says "How we see—and name—other kinds of animals matters a great deal to how we think about ourselves. … It is not their views of the world that matters here, their self naming, but how we choose to name them—as friend or foe, as similar or different."[30] It is important to consider the fact that Zwinger feels sympathy for the sheep but envisions herself in both positions, including the powerful place of the bear, where she imagines success instead of failure—which is what she actually witnessed. To summarize, Zwinger complicates our conception of bears and women in this passage because the bear is both male and female, experiences both success and failure at hunting sheep, and she characterizes all three perspectives: the bear's, the sheep's, and her own.

These complex imaginings further equate femininity with animality in a way that is different from the patriarchal version and are a subversion of the more standard conception of nonhuman animals with "otherness." This is unusual because, as Carol Adams suggests, while feminism has been busy trying to liberate women from "the onerous equation with animals and otherness, it has not disturbed the equation of animals with otherness." For Adams, "feminism" is "a species-specific philosophical system, in which (an expanded) humanity continues to negate the other animals precisely because their otherness is located in the natural sphere."[31] By associating herself and other powerful women with animals, Zwinger takes the pejorative force out of that otherwise imposed correlation and disturbs, however briefly, the equation of animals with otherness. And by including metaphors of male animality, as in the cat's cradle example, she further breaks down the metaphor's othering effect. Thus, Zwinger's move contradicts the demand by many feminists to provide new metaphors for the female relationship with nature and instead, helps us to recognize the subjectivity of animals and the agency of women in traditionally exclusionary spaces.

Feminist endeavors to provide new metaphors can lead some authors into trouble, however, as we can see in the work of Terry Tempest Williams; her attempts to equate herself and her family with animals sometimes disempowers both. Williams' repeated claim in *Refuge: An Unnatural History of Family and Place* that the local birds in her native Utah are her "relatives" is part of her effort to create an intimate relationship between herself and her environment. This effort suggests she is attempting to undo or revise the traditional conceptions of nature as a place only for men, but whereas Zwinger associates animals with subjectivity and empowerment, Williams' use of dead and dying birds to understand her mother's death inadvertently suggests that all are victims.

Williams demonstrates the connections between her mother and birds explicitly and controversially. Her mother is described as "the bird's nest behind the waterfall;"[32] facing death, "she is the bird touching both heaven and earth, flying with newfound knowledge of what it means to live."[33] Even the changes Williams anticipates in her mother's cancer-riddled body are signaled using bird imagery: "It's strange to feel change coming. It's easy to ignore. An underlying restlessness seems to accompany it like birds flocking before a storm."[34] Williams also connects specific birds with her mother's death experience. Williams' discovery of a barn swallow "who had somehow wrapped his tiny leg around the top rung of a barbed-wire fence"[35] helps her to recognize the nature of her mother's suffering. She writes of the swallow's death: "I could not leave the bird. I finally took it in my hands and unwrapped it from the wire. Its heart was racing against my fingers. The swallow had exhausted itself."[36] When it is her mother dying, Williams says, "her head was turned now, and with each breath her head drew back, reminding me of the swallow I beheld at Bear River, moments before it died."[37] These two separate stories of suffering and death, connected in this way, remind us that both the bird and Williams' mother are victims of forces outside their own power to combat. Neither has power in relation to the forceful events that take their lives; both are victims of the civilization that builds barbed-wire fences and explodes nuclear bombs in the desert. Thus, although her efforts to connect women with animals are otherwise subversive, Williams here does not redefine the traditional roles of women nor re-empower them in the face of significant environmental challenges. By emphasizing both the naturalness and the victimization of these women through her use of animal metaphors, she retains the traditional patriarchal image of both women and nature.

These two authors also experiment with different ways of describing interactive and relational connections with landscape, attempting what Arnold Berleant considers key to environmental appreciation: synaesthesia. In *The Aesthetics of Environment*, he writes, "More forcefully than in any other situation, environmental perception engages in the entire, functionally interactive human sensorium. We become part of environment through the interpenetration of body and place."[38] Williams and Zwinger try to broaden their description of environment by describing sensual interactions with the landscape, with mixed results.

In the section of her book *Red: Passion and Patience in the Desert* called "Desert Quartet," Williams writes of swimming naked: "I dissolve. I am water. Only my face is exposed like an apparition over ripples. Playing with water. Do I dare? My legs open. The rushing water turns my body and touches me with a fast finger that does not tire. I receive without apology. . . . It is endless pleasure in the current."[39]

In being so overtly and insistently sexual, the passage can be off-putting and seems an ineffective shortcut toward the embodied erotics Williams tries to articulate. In other words, if embodied erotics are, as David Abram says, "sensory interactions with the land around us,"[40] then they are far more relational than this passage suggests. Williams' message—that when we pay attention we are in a heightened state of sensitivity—becomes lost under her sexual reaction to the flowing water because instead of describing *what she is feeling*, she describes *what happens to her*. The distinction between sensual and sexual is not made in this passage, so the relationship with landscape as interactive and relational is not successfully made clear.

Zwinger endeavors to accomplish a similar point about a heightened state of bodily awareness, but she does so without depending on overly-simplified sexual imagery. She recalls an annoying dull glow in the night sky which ruins her view of the stars, and then the aurora: "Instantly, rays come down on all sides, east and west, across the entire southern sky, to the perimeters of Earth and beyond, feeding the dragons over the edge."[41] On her back, watching the sky, she says:

> I should not be as much in awe as I am. But I am. I barely breathe. The eddies and swirls get larger and larger, the magnetotail pulls out farther and farther until, like an oxbow in a river, the loops reconnect and close, separate and float off into space: the passage of vast plasmocides. . . . Cast at impossible speed for a soul without a ship, changing color from the Doppler effect, I fly inward and outward simultaneously. I remain flat on my back for several hours, not breathing, flying though space....[42]

Zwinger's sense of vertigo while watching the aurora borealis is articulated as flying: the feeling of floating or falling despite the solid ground beneath her. Her body experiences the confusion of her brain and eyes as she watches the sky glow and swirl by interpreting the signals as flying "inward and outward simultaneously." But that is not precise enough for what she feels; she expresses being overwhelmed by the light show magic even while describing it with terms for the science that makes it glow. Her sensory awe becomes her whole body's awe, overwhelming her brain's knowledge. Her interaction with the landscape occurs through all three, complicating the perceptual understanding of body and environment.

A similar "vertiginous sensation" is described in *The Last Wild Edge*, as Zwinger carefully tries to express her bodily experience with the landscape of Cape Scott on Vancouver Island. Standing at the very end of the cape, she feels "as if [she is] flying through space on a spinning ship" trailing her own electromagnetic aurora "like beautiful cobalt-purple scarves" and "as if [she is] on a thin green fur covering a strange planet, barely covered by a five-mile-thin skin of air" simultaneously.[43] She is both the mass in space and on its surface, perceiving the air above and the ground below and the awareness of her own doing so. Zwinger further becomes part of the environment in this passage as she describes the sunlit molecules buzzing her eyelids. She says, "A great feeling of safety comes over me. I am glued to this spinning ship like a limpet by an existential epoxy: symbiosis. I spread my arms and walk into the sea."[44] Her sensory interactions with landscape in her writing thus reveal her body working with the land, air, and water until language finally fails, leaving her walk into the sea up to our imaginations.

In contrast, Williams' depiction of her bodily experience with the landscape is one in which she describes herself masturbating on a rock outcropping, again funneling a broad series of physical sensations into a single response. She says:

> I stop. The silence that lives in these sacred hallways presses against me. I relax. I surrender. I close my eyes. The arousal of my breath rises in me like music, like love, as the possessive muscles between my legs tighten and release. I come to the rock in a moment of stillness, giving and receiving, where there is no partition between my body and the earth.[45]

Despite Williams' expression of the landscape "receiving" and the boundaries of body and rock dissolving, the reality is that the landscape is indifferent to her sexual pleasure.[46] So, whereas Zwinger broadens sensory perspectives, opening outward, Williams makes them internal, condensing them into bodily (and sexual) pleasure.

In another move to undermine the power of cultural and literary attitudes toward women, Zwinger is a strong and confident woman both in the roadless areas of Alaska and in the towns and cities she enters. In Central, Alaska, she acknowledges safety concerns as she enters a bar surrounded by pickup trucks with "dangerous-looking protrusions welded to front and back bumpers" but immediately feels at ease. She says,

> I take a deep breath and enter the bar; this is not always easy for me to do alone in the boonies, but this bar turns out to be an underground historical cache full of a clutter of memorabilia, pulsing, blinking, swirling beer signs, signs advising women not to wear certain items of clothes. I feel relaxed.[47]

She feels relaxed because the space, while perhaps not inviting to women, is obvious in its sexism—the signs are not really threatening because they are overt. She feels comfortable enough, in fact, to tease a man she meets there about his own gender assumptions. As he exclaims that the person who shot at his helicopter "got no balls to shoot from the rear, whoever he is," Zwinger replies, "Or she." At his quizzical look, she says, "Well, that would account for the lack of balls," and they both laugh.[48]

Her fearlessness extends to being alone in the wilderness, as well. Even as she encounters a grizzly, for example, she says, "As in most of this journey, I feel elation and heightened awareness, no fear" (80). She only articulates feeling vulnerable or fearful twice in *Stalking the Ice Dragon*. The first occasion occurs when she recognizes the vastness of the Alaskan landscape and suddenly comprehends its history:

> Up here on the Cassiar Highway, scale towers beyond human proportion. . . . The vulnerability of humankind comes through for the first time! What this *immensity* means and why we seek it. This sense of hugeness creates an understanding of our historic urge to tame: wanting to control, to impose one's own proportions throughout such tumult. A human being is insignificant here.[49]

Zwinger relates the feeling of being exposed—of feeling small in the world—with the history of exploration and conquest; while she does not condone an attitude that permits abusing the land and its inhabitants, she does acknowledge the masculine European traits motivating that desire and comprehends the incentive for Western exploitation. This first expression of vulnerability is explicitly connected to her humanity, not to her femininity in any way, although feeling vulnerable would be an understandable emotion for a woman alone in the Alaskan bush.[50]

The second time Zwinger expresses fear it is true personal fear. In a passage that allows the reader's anticipation to rise, she relates hiking up to a field:

> Then I see it!
> I freeze.
> Fear wells up in my esophagus like half-regurgitated food.
> I freeze. An animal instinct of camouflage, as if I could be invisible. So as not to be heard, I am not breathing. On the most perfect of snowfields, an orange shroud flaps violently in the wind. It could be a tent and, judging by the shape within, a hunter's body. Lying down, he fell asleep in exhaustion and now sleeps forever. . . . Its bright orange nylon beats the ground like a hummingbird heart of huge proportions.[51]

While the passage initially leaves the object of fear ambiguous, it becomes clear that Zwinger is not afraid of the tent or the hunter but of coming upon a dead body. As she approaches the flapping tent, she says, "Fear invades me like a convulsion; it enters my brain like a chemical, releases adrenaline. I am sure it will spring up to feed on me."[52] Zwinger never expresses concern about her capability around other humans, yet she is afraid of a dead body.

As she discusses her own fear about the tent's contents (which turn out to be boxes of equipment), she ponders the role of fear for men:

> I wonder if men experience the same sort of fear. No, yes, no, yes. They just call it by other names. It is the stuff their dragons are made of. Reading of John Muir traipsing his night glacial crevasses shames me. Some fears are appropriate, like fear of bear or of falling alone. Or of exposure. Or of disorientation. Such fears serve me well, to keep me safe.[53]

Even as she claims that her fear of the Orange Thing is unreasonable, it becomes plain to us that it actually brings all her fears together—the risk of being mauled, of falling without hope of rescue, of becoming lost. The flapping orange tent, scarred by bear claws, marks the land with all her fear. Notice, however, that fear of men is not one of them. Her fears are universal ones. Although she describes her concerns about traveling alone in a desolate landscape, she does so through the lens of humanity, not the apprehension, however reasonable, resulting from a history of violence against femininity. She changes perspectives from that of a *woman* traveling alone to that of a *human* traveling alone.

Just as Zwinger claims she wants to change perspective in relation to the landscapes she experiences, she broadens our conceptions of the world through her narrative choices, and Williams similarly strives to create new metaphors for her relationship with landscape. Both authors are subversive for the way they complicate typical notions of women, animals, and nature, revealing all to be members of a beautiful intertwined community. These women show that mourning a lost wilderness is not as fruitful as reconsidering what wilderness is—full of civilization, like tents and other people. Zwinger seems most successful at encouraging a change in behavior toward the environment because she treats nature as more than a fragile object that needs saving. She reveals how a mind and body engaged with the world can expose what is left invisible in most explorations into nature—practical concerns, women, other people, other animals—showing us how nature and culture really interact. Thus, these two women, writing about nature, provide a basis for the reconstruction of the concept of nature itself by integrating the interests of actual women into an actual wilderness, and one that is not simply a feminine metaphor.

Notes

1. The few exceptions make this claim even stronger: an examination of online "Introduction to Nature Writing" syllabi reveals that there are only three women authors regularly named: Mary Austin, Rachel Carson, and Terry Tempest Williams.

2. William Cronon, "The Trouble with Wilderness: or, Getting Back to the Wrong Nature," in *Uncommon Ground: Rethinking the Human Place in Nature*, ed. William Cronon (New York: Norton, 1996), 78.

3. Annette Kolodny, *The Land Before Her: Fantasy and Experience of the American Frontiers, 1630-1860* (Chapel Hill: University of North Carolina Press, 1984), 3.

4. Of course there are other forms of nature writing in America, most recently rural and suburban writing. For example, works by Janisse Ray, Robert Winkler, Peter Friederici, Lisa Couturier, and Jennifer Price all examine environments close to home—and certainly desire to redefine "wilderness" and "nature." I'm most interested in the Throeauvian mode of nature writing here, however. I should also note that there is some recent scholarship about the solitary male adventurer in nature (including the collection *Eco-Man: New Perspectives on Masculinity and Nature* edited by Mark Allister), but I am not convinced that new examinations of the comfortable role men can assume in wilderness are necessarily a progressive or beneficial move when it comes to invalidating the limitations that are placed on women in nature.

5. Susan Zwinger, *The Last Wild Edge: One Woman's Journey from the Arctic Circle to the Olympic Rain Forest* (Colorado: Johnson Books, 1999), xi.

6. Zwinger, *The Last Wild Edge*, xii.

7. Zwinger, *The Last Wild Edge*, xii.

8. Susan Zwinger, *Stalking the Ice Dragon: An Alaskan Journey* (Tucson: University of Arizona Press, 1991), xi.

9. Zwinger, *Stalking the Ice Dragon*, 10.

10. Zwinger, *Stalking the Ice Dragon*, 24.

11. Zwinger, *Stalking the Ice Dragon*, 25.

12. Zwinger, *Stalking the Ice Dragon*, 3.

13. Zwinger, *Stalking the Ice Dragon*, 12.

14. Zwinger, *Stalking the Ice Dragon,*, 119.

15. Zwinger, *Stalking the Ice Dragon.*, xii.

16. Zwinger, *Stalking the Ice Dragon*, 7.

17. Josephine Donovan, "Animal Rights and Feminist Theory," in *Ecofeminism: Women, Animals, Nature*, ed. Greta Gaard (Philadelphia: Temple University Press, 1993), 175.

18. Carol J. Adams, "Feminist Traffic in Animals," in *Ecofeminism: Women, Animals, Nature*, ed. Greta Gaard (Philadelphia: Temple University Press, 1993), 204.

19. Kate Soper, *What is Nature?* (Oxford: Blackwell Publishers, 1995), 123.

20. Louise Westling, *The Green Breast of the New World: Landscape, Gender, and American Fiction* (Athens: University of Georgia Press, 1993),167.

21. Lynda Birke, *Feminism, Animals, Science: The Naming of the Shrew* (Buckingham: Open University Press, 1994), 38.

22. Zwinger, *Stalking*, 79.

23. Zwinger, *Stalking*, 80.

24. Barney Nelson, *The Wild and the Domestic: Animal Representation, Ecocriticism, and Western American Literature* (Reno: University of Nevada Press, 2000), 54.

25. Zwinger, *Stalking*, 81.

26. Donna Haraway, *Primate Visions: Gender, Race, and Nature in the World of Modern Science* (New York: Routledge, 1989), 196.

27. Margaret Homans, *Bearing the Word: Language and Female Experience in Nineteenth-Century Women's Writing* (Chicago: University of Chicago Press, 1986), 63.This effort is something Dana Phillips ridicules in his recent book, *The Truth of Ecology: Nature, Culture, and Literature in America*. He argues that "ecocritics who want the world to be in the text often describe environmental literature as a kind of writing, in the narrow sense of *inscription*, which bears little of the freight associated with traditional genres and forms. . . . [E]cocritics are inclined to interpret [nature writing] as if it were veritably a form of writing degree zero, as indeed it often tries to be" (15). While there is some truth in Phillips' position generally, it is an overly-simplified way to consider specific texts. In this case, there is a difference between traditional narrative and the passages Zwinger uses to connect her readers with her experience. She does not merely say, "I saw some sheep behaving strangely and discovered the cause was a bear." She forces her readers to feel sensory confusion before discovering the cause, just as she did during the actual, non-narrative event. As Arnold Berleant says in his work on the aesthetics of environment, "Perceiving environment occurs in many ways and on many different levels. It moves from the fleeting recognition of cues that provide practical information to the specialized study of natural phenomena" (*The Aesthetics of Environment* 14). By imitating this fullness of perception, Zwinger's passages move from visual and physical confusion to recognition. By emphasizing her direct engagement with the scene before her, Zwinger reduces the pressure of cultural factors in her representation of other animals. Counter to Phillips' claims, she maintains the sense of her own bodiliness and psychological and physiological confusion in her literary representation of the scene.

28. Zwinger, *Stalking*, 81.

29. Zwinger, *Stalking*, 82.

30. Birke, 16.

31. Adams, 204.

32. Terry Tempest Williams, *Refuge: An Unnatural History of Family and Place* (New York: Vintage Books, 1991), 61.

33. Williams, *Refuge*, 136.

34. Williams, *Refuge*, 24.

35. Williams, *Refuge*, 52.

36. Williams, *Refuge*, 53.

37. Williams, *Refuge*, 230.

38. Arnold Berleant, *The Aesthetics of Environment* (Philadelphia: Temple University Press, 1992), 16-7.

39. Terry Tempest Williams, *Red: Passion and Patience in the Desert* (New York: Random House, 2001), 201.

40. David Abram, "Turning Inside Out," *Orion* 15, no. 1 (1996): 56.

41. Zwinger, *Stalking*, 182.

42. Zwinger, *Stalking*, 183.

43. Zwinger, *The Last Wild Edge*, 124, 125.

44. Zwinger, *The Last Wild Edge*, 125.

45. Williams, *Red*, 197.

46. For a different reading of this passage, see Sharon A. Reynolds' essay "Beyond Mere Embrace in *Desert Quartet: An Erotic Landscape*." There Reynolds argues that Williams "makes a practice of reshaping the metaphors representing our personal connections to the American West's expansive landscape, often challenging persistent fantasies of the land as plentiful virgin territory to be ravished" (47). Using the assertion of Vera Norwood and Janice Monk that women's relationships with landscape are based on reciprocity and personal vulnerability rather than heroic dominance (*The Desert is No Lady* 234), Reynolds suggests that Williams strives to "merge with the unknown" (51) in acts of vulnerability that are positive. Yet I find that Williams' "merging" is actually one of her solitary sexual satisfaction, strongly reminiscent of the sexual metaphors used to "ravish" the landscape. Her behavior is only risky in terms of cultural norms that suggest masturbation with rocks and water is inappropriate; it does not reflect a personal vulnerability toward the landscape itself. In contrast, I argue that Zwinger's elaborate and complicated bodily response to the landscape and aurora borealis does express an effort toward a merging with the unknown.

47. Zwinger, *Stalking*, 36.

48, Zwinger, *Stalking*, 39.

49. Zwinger, *Stalking*, 9.

50. Such vulnerability would be an outgrowth of violence perpetuated toward women, not one that rewrites the tradition of the land being unavailable to women (which that violence perpetuates). This circularity means that as long as the notion of vulnerability is firmly attached to the risk of bodily harm at the hands of other humans, it is not a move toward powerfully embodied femininity, so it is important to also recognize the ways in which Zwinger and Williams both rewrite that history by not submitting to it.

51. Zwinger, *Stalking*, 138.

51. Zwinger, *Stalking*, 139.

53. Zwinger, *Stalking*, 139.

6

Louise Gluck, Feminism and Nature in *Firstborn*'s "The Egg"

Mary Kate Azcuy

In her initial collection *Firstborn* (1968), Contemporary, American poet Louise Gluck's three-part poem "The Egg" progresses through three scenes that introduce the questions and answers that define Gluck's lifelong understanding of and relationship to the environment and the mythic as she redefines *feminine*[1] via detailed, poetic landscape images. The observer, Gluck, moves beyond gender limits assigned to feminine space by western, patriarchal traditions, including maternal paganism and a Judeo-Christian paradigm, all of which Gluck deconstructs in order to transcend such limiting cultural parameters. This transcendence moves women back outside into nature, a now empowered *feminine* space, to reclaim the garden and sea, find healing from trauma, and discover spirituality.

Outside, in nature, Gluck's poetry joins third-wave feminism's ecofeminism, in addressing an environment destabilized by male domination, similar to the oppressive treatment of women in western society.[2] Gluck further destabilizes the environment and uses that to show a nature/culture interrelationship while exposing issues in reproductive rights.[3] These ecofeministic issues promote earth awareness, a redefined feminine-earth power, and a feminine and earthly divinity that moves beyond the "limits" assigned by men, as women recreate a powerful connection to nature.[4]

Gluck's ecofeminist poetry involves the interrelationship between the human, feminine, and non-human, earth and sea. "The Egg" deconstructs and reimages western ideas of objects, such as the egg, and places, earth, garden, and sea. Gluck uses the images of earth and water to confess abortion, come to terms with shame, and find self-understanding as a woman facing such memories.[5]

Gluck begins balancing the story of her life and the ideas in the egg, the object that transmits her story. She comments that in "refocusing an existing image of the world; in this sense, it is less mirror than microscope."[6] In her re-visioning and cautioning to readers against using her images as a measure purely of her life, her work moves past any simple biographical concerns to question situations and constructions of the feminine in universal terms. In *Proofs & Theories* she clarifies the question of self-revelation in poetry: "Poems are autobiography, but divested of the trappings of chronology and comment. . . . Moreover, a body of work may change and develop less in reaction to the lived life than in reaction to the poet's prior discoveries, or the discoveries of others. . . . And if, in its striving to be free of the imprisoning self, the poet's gaze trains itself outward, . . . Such choices constitute a portrait."[7]

Gluck looks to nature and observes that the earthly, poetic focus "for our century has been to substitute earth for god as an object of reverence."[8] However, Gluck does not choose to be identified or labeled a "nature-poet" because she is offended by male poets' ideals of "maternal paganism."[9] Maggie Gordon agrees that Gluck is part of an ecofeminist movement, ordered by Francoise d'Eaubonne in *Le Feminisme ou la mort* showing "the interdependence of human and nonhuman nature" in relation to "human bodily nature" and "physical and psychological experience."[10] Gluck meets the revolutionary challenge and joins the human and non-human and "the shared materiality of the personal and earth bodies that leads to the use of a myth-narrative lyric."[11] In accordance with d'Eaubonne's "Que pourrait être une société écofeministe?" ("What Could an Ecofeminist Society Be?") and third-wave ecofeminism, Gluck moves beyond male/female dualism to an "abolition of patriarchy and the establishment of a relationship with the environment that is finally balanced."[12]

Balance in the new feminine environment can occur only after the original becomes disrupted; the female images associated with woman, womb, earth, and sea, must be taken from patriarchy and transformed, recreated, not as anti-motherhood, but as female space. These reconstructed places/spaces follow the feminist reclaiming of Edenic landscapes, after female banishment.[13] For Gluck, ultimately, the earth survives as the female Other,[14] yet Other beyond the primordial egg and womb to recreation, where Gluck's shame and rage perish and replenish the earth, the earth that represents her.

Earth, creation, and recreation images arrive in "The Egg" and function to display complex metaphors. The three-part poem follows three life phases associated by Leo Tolstoy: Youth's search for comprehension details loss, here, the loss of love and life creates a new female identity; Middle life questions one's own culpability, here, entwined in female guilt regarding abortion, this poem's complex metaphor; foreshadowing Age and its related spiritual quest, Gluck does not move to religious traditions for comfort but deeper into a "new" feminine environment in nature. In "The Egg," Youth's voice and search to comprehend a male lover's disregard and the mother-child's betrayal to the now aborted fetus, all seems to premonitor the comprehension and spiritual understanding from nature that encompass Gluck's life-long work. In the initiating journey, Youth's voice searches for salvation lost to her, as she now searches for comprehension of lost love. Throughout this poem's painful re-experience, Gluck moves away from trauma into the natural scene to find spiritual recovery.[15]

For Gluck, the patriarchal tradition of God does not comfort, but alienates. During "The Egg" Part I, she travels with her family on vacation, aware that a male God will not save her:

Everything went in the car.
Slept in the car, slept
Like angels in the duned graveyards,
Being gone. . . .[16]

The children travel as God's victims, "angels in the duned graveyards."[17] Gluck searches, in memory, in the darkness of the vacationing family's car. She understands that God and her lover's abandonment connect to the secret abortion. Love and life are lost and dead like packaged food that rots; "A week's meat / Spoiled" as the unborn, baby "peas / Giggled in their pods" innocent to their awaiting water-deaths, symbolic of her own destroyed egg moving into water.[18] Shattered, tainted Gluck draws images of innocence, yet understands that death carries abortion's haunting secret. The innocents do not navigate the voyage but are the unborn eggs that cannot return: "I heard my insides / Roll into a crib . . . ."[19] With innocence gone, the idea of a sleeping child, self or the aborted, now equal lost "ideals," deconstructed traditional images.

Here, Gluck discloses the aborted child; the word "washing" implies the emptying womb and aborted tissue and blood into the ocean: "Washing underwear in the Atlantic."[20] She expels her lost innocence; the bleeding womb disturbs traditional ideas attributed to seaside vacations, seascapes, and a nurturing womb. The hurt young woman moves into the ocean's water to cleanse her actions and the consequences. The landscape tradition rattles as beauty and pristine nature unify with 20th century circumstance and reality, a young woman hiding the secret and resulting shame of abortion. Gluck's work does not embrace anti-motherhood; although, she often uses metaphors of destructive mother relations to examine her own difficult interactions with her mother. Here Gluck disrupts the tradition that Helene Cixous identifies as the male attributions of woman that encompass "mother and other," while Gluck uses this poem to explore the "subversive and disruptive potential" of changes to those perceptions.[21]

French feminist Luce Irigaray looks at the duality of the situation for womb and Other in finding the womb a receptacle: not individual, female, but the recipient of male desire where "The Other serves as matrix / womb for the subject's signifiers; such would be the cause of its desire."[22] Yet, the desire and resulting displacement of the young woman move her away from a victim's position and returns an empowered female image. The deconstructed egg joins the vast earth's womb, the sea and water, with images of roundness. The womb that

Luce Irigaray finds suppressive to women, now conveys the literal womb's extractions and regenerates in rejoining death into nurturing future life, where nature heals: Touched the sun's sea / As light welled / That could devour water.[23] Nature can embrace the "lost" as the earth and sun absorb water, the displaced. Gluck connects the aborted fetus, empty womb, water to nature and the sun, while she battles the idea of womb as receptacle, dispels all contact, and returns life-giving and death forces/fluids to earth and water.[24]

Gluck confesses to purge suffering and in this catharsis frees self and feminine to heal. She contains the vastness of the story within mythic proportions: Earth becomes relative to mother, Gaia, and blood returns to water, the implied Furies' justice becomes the burden of guilt, born from (Ouranos) patriarchy's blood. Many feminist theorists draw conclusions regarding the myth of earth relative to male domination. Simone de Beauvoir discussed the mythological imbalance for women and the discomfort female power evokes in men, in the earth-mother's digestion of her children's remains. (The Fury warning includes punishment to matriarchal figures involved in *infanticide*.) Gluck's symbolic femicide does not focus on female-pagan systems, but adds ancient Judeo-Christian patriarchal systems (the burdening Eve and empty-wombed Mary); thus, myth joins the postmodern and the ancient.[25]

Now that Gluck has disrupted the images, a new understanding comes from the past. In some ancient rite, blood returns as fertility and honor to enrich earth and continues to justify mother, moving beyond traditional attributes. Gluck's re-imaging in water stands in a quandary between a strong idea of patriarchal punishment and healing rebirth, through her own mock baptism, as she moves into the water.[26]

In Part II, the mature Middle-life voice finds death, as the poet unveils the abortion scene and details the consequences of and connections between male and female. In surreal, ethereal memory Gluck recalls the abortionist and remains passive in the act:

> The sterilizer his enormous hands
> Swarmed, carnivorous,
> For prey . . . .[27]

The mythological tradition of the scene shifts: Blame of abortion moves to the hands of the male, aggressive in contact with female genitalia yet removing the male remains of copulation. Yet, he still inserts a phallus into the womb, "Open to the wand"[28]— here the abortionist's wand. This place, scene, reconstructs the destroyed male/female relationship. In destruction comes renewal in newness of place.

This new vision and complex metaphor involve a new "Feminist Ethics,"[29] as Gluck decides to move toward comprehension, beyond consequence, toward healing in her space. At her most vulnerable, yet lucid, she absorbs the scene and sees the mirroring reflection of her exposed body:

Dripping white, stripped
Open to the wand,
I saw the lamps
Converging in his glasses.[30]

Mirror images reflect Gluck's image.[31] Gluck understands the creation of a passive/female and aggressive/male conundrum and finds culpability with her rejecting partner and questions his occupation in the deed: ". . . You let him / Rob me."[32]

Drugged and "robbed" of "child," provides anonymous distance to envision the procedure: Past cutlery I saw / My body stretching like a tear / Along the paper.[33] The traditional female purpose, as mother, feels irreversibly lost to the action and inactions of males, the Mary figure lost to physicality void of choice in conception and power. Here, alienated from love, Gluck comprehends the scene.[34]

In Part III, a distanced Gluck moves into her mature, future vision, the poet who observes nature and the landscape. Fear and memory reemerge and morph with images outside in nature that need to further dissipate. She recalls her union with the rejecting male:

Always nights I feel the ocean
Biting at my life. By
Inlet, in this net
Of bays, and on. Unsafe.
And on, numb
In the bourbon ripples
Of your breath
I knot . . . [35]

This male lover represents a Christian, patriarchal symbol that now joins the waste of nature and nature's life-death process. The idea of male power associated with the One, the divine-male power / God figure.[36]

Now, "The Egg" moves to further deconstruct as fish (drawing from the Christian, womb-shaped symbol) arrive. Carcasses and fragments of fish move across the water in moonlight:

Across the beach the fish
Are coming in. Without skins,
Without fins, the bare
Households of their skulls
Still fixed, piling
With the other waste.
Husks, husks. Moons
Whistle in their mouths,
Through gasping mussels.
Pried flesh. And flies[37]

Images remind in art that not all of life survives and that patriarchal Christian traditions obliterate in moonlight's quiet, underground clarity. These images also relate destruction to the environment, created under the stewardship of the dominant gender. The fish flesh has been pried away from bones and shells in nature like the child from the cusp of womb in choice. The young girl laments and confronts lost constructions, innocence, her own, her potential child's, and questions life after such obliterations.

Nature provides Gluck with answers at a point in transformation where the seascape embraces nature's beauty: Like planets, clamped shells / Clink blindly through / Veronicas of waves . . . [38] Simultaneously, grotesque images move toward recreation in understanding the "bones" of essence and truth:

> The thing
> Is hatching. Look. The bones
> Are bending to give way.
> It's dark. It's dark.[39]

In Jungian shadows, Gluck sees her anorexic self, her unwanted body image like the fish stripped of flesh that ties back to male treatment of females and the environment, aborted psyches, as well as her own battle to heal from suffering, her break with lover, mother, and sibling loss, the self, skeletal bits and pieces.

Worlds blend as night joins life and death and spirit in the three ages of Gluck.[40] The insufferable, intolerable, and maddening memories and situations find purgation in the seascape where suffering and imagination meet in a postmodern, post-Christian, ecofeminist blurring of the lines.

What begins to reform must find its way back to the beginning in the cycle, the roundness of life.[41] The inherent roundness in the world creates natural attachments.[42] Gluck searches images of roundness in womb, moon, and egg to relate back to earth and healing. As another possible egg moves into the poem, the hatching, a possible recreation from the past must end.

The hatching ends in memory of the abortion and the destruction of the patriarchal past: "He's brought a bowl to catch / The pieces of the baby."[43] The future creation waits. New life cannot exist until new terms exist for the past. Gluck's re-creation does not come in new life but in finding identity for self and women in what exists, feminine space. Gluck parallels her understanding of the scene to the abortionist's deed, now catching "pieces of the baby" he's destroyed. The deconstructed can be reshaped from the observer's guilt that matches nature's destruction and unpredictable chaos. Living things die and sea life breaks apart like the lover that meant nothing, the aborted baby (woman-child, self), and random fish pieces.[44] After recognition of shame and suffering, Gluck must fill the void beyond the obvious construction of femaleness and motherhood.

"The Egg" searches nature to find hope, despite guilt, to comprehend betrayal to the aborted fetus and the betrayal to her by an absent lover. She suffers in this topic.[45] As Gluck's poetry searches for the "dead child," she creates poem in this topic. As Gluck's poetry searches for the "dead child," she creates poem after poem trying to understand what occurred in her Youth. Her poetic usage demonstrates Sartre's claim that people resort to art/genius "'in desperate circumstances.'"[46]

Lee Upton says Gluck associates herself with suffering in women and initially wanted to write of death and the abandoned,[47] yet she tries to alienate the body from the earth, rejects traditional female qualities and clichés, and focuses on alienation for contemporary females versus inclusion by "Other"/males. Her abortion image represents her struggles[48] to find these new realms, and in this representative work defines the plan for her life's work. Gluck's poems often center in the garden, a location she embraces and understands, yet, she warns about the return to the archetypal "Garden" when the real ideal is to move beyond the "dark matter," the exile and punishment where the female-tragic image remains trapped.[49] Instead, the ambition is to move to a new ideal, not returning but transcending.[50]

"The Egg" initiates the three phases in which her work and life will journey. She uses the metaphor and situation of abortion to dispel loss and disconnection (mother/child, male/female, self), as Gluck observes loss, death, and potential recreation in a post-Judeo-Christian nature. This poem moves beyond Eve's prostration and beyond the virgin womb of Mary. Gluck transcends these these limits to a new and powerful ecofeminist revisioning in nature.

Notes

1. Krista Ratcliffe relates *feminine* as "behaviors grounded in socially constructed gender differences" (7).

2. Rosemary Radford Ruether, "Ecofeminism: Symbolic and Social Connection of the Oppression of Women and the Domination of Nature," *Ecofeminism and the Sacred*, ed. Carol J. Robb (New York: Crossroad Books, 1993), 13-23. Ruether writes that in the roots of ecofeminism are involved in the "symbolic connections of domination of women and domination of nature in Mediterranean and Western European culture" (22).

3. This evokes Foucault's idea of resistance.

4. Note Irene Diamond and Gloria Feman Orenstien's ideas involving criteria in *Reweaving the World: The Emergence of Ecofeminism* (San Francisco: Sierra Books, 1990), xii-xiii.

5. My uses of the pronouns her/she are referent to the poem's female speaker.

6. Louise Gluck, *Proofs & Theories* (New Jersey: Ecco Press, 1994), 93.

7. Gluck, *Proofs & Theories*, 92.

8. Gluck, *Proofs & Theories*, 21.

9. Maggie Gordon. "A Woman Writing about Nature: Louise Gluck and 'the absence of intention.'" *Ecopoetry: A Critical Introduction*. ed. J. Scott Bryson (Salt Lake City: University of Utah Press, 2002), 222.

10. Gordon. "A Woman Writing about Nature," 222.

11. Gordon. "A Woman Writing About Nature," 223.

12. Francoise d'Eaubonne's "What Could an Eco-Feminist Society Be?" *Liberty, Equality and Women?* Jacob Paisain, trans. *Ethics and the Environment*, 4 (2):179-184.

13. Mary Daly, in *Gyn/Ecology: The Metaethics of Radical Feminism* (Boston: Beacon, 1990) envisions such landscapes: "A primary definition of paradise is 'pleasure park.' The walls of the Patriarchal Pleasure Park represent the condition of being perpetually parked, locked into the parking lot of the past. . . . Patriarchal Paradise is the arena of games, the place where the pleas of women are silenced, where the law is: Please the Patrons. Women who break through the imprisoning walls of the Playboys' Playground are entering the process which is our happenings/happiness. This is Paradise beyond the boundaries of 'paradise'" (7).

14. Locked in patriarchy's dissatisfaction, women remain trapped, as Simone de Beauvoir's identified Other.

15. Gluck finds similarity in T.S. Eliot's work: "What has driven these poems from the first is terror and need of the understandable other. When the terror becomes unbearable, the other becomes god" (*Proofs* 22).

16. Louise Gluck, "The Egg," *Firstborn* (1968): *The First Four Books of Poems.* (New Jersey: Ecco Press, 1995), 6.

17. Gluck, "The Egg," 6.

18. Gluck, "The Egg," 6.

19. Gluck, "The Egg," 6.

20. Gluck, "The Egg," 6.

21. Helene Cixous, "Sorties: Out and Out: attacks/ways out/forays," (1975) and "The laugh of the Medusa" (1975), quoted in Michael Payne, ed. *Cultural and Critical Theory.* Oxford, UK: Blackwell, 2001, 104.

22. Luce Irigaray. "Cosi Fan Tutti." *The Sex Which is Not One*. trans. Catherine Porter and Carolyn Burke Ithaca, N.Y. : Cornell UP, 1985, 101.

23. Gluck "The Egg" 6.

24. Irigaray's "The 'Mechanics' of Fluids," *This Sex Which is Not One*, C. Porter and C. Burke, trans., (Ithaca and New York: Cornell University Press, 1985) discusses the problematic image of female and the womb as receptacle for the male.

25. Eva Feder Kittany's "Woman as Metaphor," *Feminist Social Thought*, Diana Tietjens Meyers, ed. (New York and London: Routledge, 1997) relates the power imbalance specifically regarding the water image that suffers in its duality as "the life-giving yet fearsome powers of a female Sea, the welcoming and enveloping or suffocating and confining" (271).

26. Post-Christian theologian and feminist scholar Daphne Hampson, *After Christianity* (London: SCM Press, 2002), relates to the feminine dilemma in her observation of the doors to the baptistery at Piazza del Duomo, which depict Abraham's attack on Isaac, a similar, irony in Gluck's counterpoints of mother and abortion's remains returning into the water in a baptismal tradition: "What an odd choice, one might think, of a scene. . . . That is, until one recognizes, first, that baptism is the ceremony which marks the entry into the world of the male religion, displacing as it does the natural birth from a woman, and furthermore, that the story . . . may well mark the securing of patriarchy in a (male) God-father-son genealogy. . . Feminism is the interpretative perspective which we have lacked" (87).

27. Hampson, *After Christianity*, 87.

28. Hampson, *After Christianity*, 7.

29. As proposed by Hampson, who cites Roger Poole's work *Towards Deep Subjectivity*, (New York and London: Harper Torch Books, 1972) regarding new generations and space: "Every age has its characteristic conceptual space . . . Every thinker brings a space into being which he establishes as peculiarly his own . . . Just how one wins through to a space one can think in involves a very interesting series of

conceptual transformations . . . The thinker shapes himself as he thinks. He excludes or includes, he modifies the shape of his world. Philosophical space is thus the space of choice. The thinker has to decide not only what is right and wrong but also what he wants to *become* by deciding what he wants to become, he decides indirectly what he wants his world to become."

30. Gluck 'The Egg" 7

31. Jacques Lacan, from "Mirror Stage," would find the "identificatory effect produced by images and movements of others of the same species and even images and movements which merely *simulate* those of the species in question . . . [creating] the origin of an organism's orientation toward its own species. . . . the mirror stage that allows him, . . . cultural specificity of body images" (qtd. in Moira Gatens, "Power, Bodies and Difference," *Destabilizing Theory,* Michele Barrett and Anne Phillips, eds. (Stanford, CA: Stanford University Press, 1992), 131).

32. Gluck "The Egg" 7.

33. Gluck "The Egg" 7.

34. Gluck "The Egg" 102.

35. Gluck "The Egg" 8.

36. Irigaray comments on transitory, physical unions of imbalance, stating that true pleasure comes in equity, but in imbalance the male finds "narcissistic pleasure" as ". . .the master, believing himself to be unique, [and] confuses with that of the One" (103).

37. Gluck "The Egg" 8.

38. Gluck "The Egg" 8.

39. Gluck "The Egg" 8.

40. Spiritual poet Jane Hirshfield identifies the area where worlds blend as "what difficult to see . . . the realms of sorrow, chaos, indeterminacy, anger . . . " that writers use "to seek out the places where madness and imagination meet" *Nine Gates: Entering the Mind of Poetry.* (New York: Harper, 1997). 5.

41. Gaston Bachelard devotes a chapter of *The Poetics of Space* (Boston: Beacon Press, 1964, 1994) to roundness relative to Karl Jaspers' "*Jedes Dasein scheint in sich rund* (Every being seems in itself round)" (232).

42. Bachelard, *The Poetics of Space*, 232.

43. Gluck "The Egg" 8.

44. In Gluck's discussion of Rilke's use of voids, she understands that after emptiness comes newness: "In the broken thing, moreover, human agency is oddly implied: breakage, whatever its cause, is the dark complement to the act of making; the one implies the other. The thing that is broken has particular authority over the act of change. Rilke's poem begins with the unknowable, a void located in the past. And ends with the unknown: a new, a different, life; a void projected into the future" (*Proofs* 75).

45. Jane Hirshfield, *Nine Gates: Entering the Mind of Poetry.*(New York: Harper, 1997). She recognizes this as the artistic search for truth and knows that "there are times when suffering's only open path is through an immersion in what is" (5).

46. Hirshfield, *Nine Gates.* 5.

47. Lee Upton, "Fleshless Voices: Louise Gluck's Rituals of Abjection and Oblivion," *The Muse of Abandonment: Origin, Identity, Mastery in Five American Poets* (Lewisburg: Bucknell University Press, 1998), 120.

48. Upton "Fleshless Voices" 122.

49. Gluck *Proofs* 53.

50. Gluck *Proofs* 53.

7

Ecofeminism, Motherhood, and the Post-Apocalyptic Utopia in *Parable of the Sower*, *Parable of the Talents*, and *Into the Forest*

Heidi Hutner

We have a beautiful
Mother
Her green lap
immense
Her brown embrace
Eternal
Her blue body
Everything
We know . . .
—*Alice Walker, Her Blue Body Everything We know*

There is nothing alien
About nature,
Nature
Is all that exists.
It's the earth
And all that's on it.
It's the universe...
—Octavia Butler, *Parable of the Talents*

Octavia Butler's *Parable of the Sower*, its sequel, *Parable of the Talents*, and Jean Hegland's *Into the Forest*, link the domination of nature with the exploitation and oppression of women. As Karen J. Warren writes, "important connections exist between the treatment of women, people of color, and the underclass on one hand and the treatment of nonhuman nature on the other."[1] In *Sower, Talents,* and *Forest*, Butler and Hegland attempt to solve the problem of ecological devastation and the oppression of women (and "others"—for Butler) with the creation of utopian feminized societies based on what Carolyn Merchant calls an egalitarian "partnership ethic" between the "human community and nonhuman nature."[2] Both Butler and Hegland seek redemption in tales of new worlds—outside of their violent and corrupt dystopian cultures. For Butler, this *somewhere else* is on other planets; for Hegland, it is in the forest in an idealized female hunter-gatherer society.

In *Reinventing Eden*, Merchant examines those who would seek an idealistic prelapsarian vision in "reinventing paradise" throughout history. She critiques these reinventions of Eden and offers a "partnership ethic" as an alternative to such a potentially damaging narrative. "For many Americans," writes Merchant, "humanity's loss of the perfect Garden of Eden is among the most powerful of stories. Consciously at times, unconsciously at others, we search for ways to reclaim our loss. . . . But "mastering" nature to reclaim Eden has nearly destroyed the very nature people have tried to reclaim."[3] What Merchant describes are two primary visions of nature's history—the version that supports the position that mankind has the right to dominate nature, women, and others, and the declensionist version, held by post-modernists, environmentalists, and feminists, who believe nature is fallen, and that human beings have exploited and denigrated nature. Merchant calls upon us in the present to develop what she describes as an interdependent partnership with the natural world.[4] This partnership ethic includes the following precepts:

> *Equity between the human and nonhuman communities
> *Moral consideration for both humans and other species
> *Respect for both cultural diversity and biodiversity
> *Inclusion of women, minorities, and nonhuman nature in the code of ethical accountability
> *An ecologically sound management that is consistent with the continued health of both the human and the nonhuman communities[5]

In effect, Merchant's partnership ethic is founded on a "relational" concept of "care."[6] It "is an ethic based on the idea that people are helpers, partners and colleagues and that people and nature are equally important to each other." This is a "mutually beneficial situation[,]" Merchant states, "[l]ike the Native-American idea of a sacred bundle of relationships and obligations, a partnership ethic is grounded in the ideas of relation and of mutual obligation. . . .Like human partners, the earth and humanity communicate with each other."[7]

In this essay I want to expand Merchant's partnership ethic to include the discourses of mothering, as mothers and "mother-nature" are ambivalently rendered by Butler and Hegland, and they figure complexly in the relationship between humans and nonhumans in these novels. Typical of much ecofeminist "mother-earth" rhetoric, where mothers and nature are constructed symbiotically and women become in danger of being essentialized as nurturers,[8] both the maternal figures and nature are abused in these works. Yet this structure is complicated by Butler and Hegland, as the mothers in *The Parables* and *Forest* are blamed for the daughters' crises in the post-apocalyptic world, and they are portrayed as being "unnaturally" and "monstrously" distanced from the natural environment *and* their children. These novels question what happens when mothers are not conventional nurturers, and/or when they do not put nature first.

The matriphobic crises in *The Parables* and *Forest* draw on an ideology of "intensive mothering" which, as Andrea O'Reilly describes, involves an absolute denial of the mother's identity apart from her child. The intensive (biological) mother must be fully involved with her child at all times—to the exclusion of all other tasks, including work outside the home, domestic labor within the home, and all relationships with those other than her children. These demands result in the denial and "sublimation of the mother's own selfhood and . . . agency, autonomy, authenticity, and authority." As O'Reilly argues, the ideology of intensive mothering functions as "backlash discourse" that "regulate[s]" women and constructs all mothers as "failures."[9]

In *Sower* and *Talents*, the protagonist, Lauren, is trapped within the dichotomy of Good/Bad mother O'Reilly's work articulates; she cannot be an intense biological mother figure and a successful environmental and political visionary at the same time. However, in *The Parables,* there is a space for communal mothering, as Patricia Hill Collins (and, many others, such as bell hooks) delineate it in a black female sociological context, within Butler's utopia.[10] Communal mothering (and/or parenting) functions subversively in the novels, and this allows Lauren's unconventional mode of mothering to extend beyond her own biological child to the community at large. For Hegland, the figure of the mother is dangerously distanced from her relationship with nature; later, as mother(s) themselves, the daughters must learn to reconnect with mother earth, and thus they heal both the discordant mother/child bonds as well as the bonds between human and nonhuman nature. Indeed, for Hegland, the partnership ethic is enacted simultaneously as an ideal that might resemble partnership mothering, as well as a human reconnection with nature and the nonhuman world.

Parable of the Sower begins in 2024 in the suburban community of Robledo, twenty miles outside of Los Angeles. The dystopic world is in social, moral, and civil disorder; and the walled-in cul-de-sac community where the fifteen-year old Lauren, the protagonist and narrator lives, is only temporarily safe from the dangers that rage through the outside city.[11] As Peter Stillman, among others, points out, the novel's dystopian vision exemplifies the intensified ideologies of the "Reagan years" and the "Republican right."[12] *Sower* is filled with racial separatism, patriarchal oppression, violence, and environmental degradation. Drug addicts and pyromaniacs called "paints" attack and murder ruthlessly, women are raped repeatedly, and the streets are riddled with corpses, naked bodies, homeless people, and wild dogs that attack and kill humans. There are frequent abductions as well, and people are taken into slavery—sexual and otherwise. As Jim Miller states, the novel "outlines the impact of class polarizations on a local, national, and international level. . . .[T]he rich are out of the picture, above the fray, as the middle class and the desperate poor fight over an ever-shrinking pie."[13]

In the midst of this dystopian socio-economic chaos, the late-capitalist world is in an environmental crisis on multiple levels. Sylvia Mayer aptly argues that, "Butler confirms the basic notion of the environmental justice movement that social and environmental justice are indivisible," as *The Parables* focus on a Black female narrator and low-income, marginalized, and oppressed groups.[14] Clean water, for example, is a much sought-after commodity, particularly for the middle class and the poor. Lauren explains the plight of her situation:

> The cost of water has gone up again. And I heard on the news today that more water peddlers are being killed. Peddlers sell water to squatters and the street poor—and to people who have managed to hold on to their homes but not to pay their utility bills. Peddlers are being found with their throats cut and their money and their hand trucks stolen. Dad says water now costs several times as much as gasoline. But except for arsonists and the rich, most people have given up buying gasoline . . . It's a lot harder to give up water.[15]

"[P]eople have changed the climate of the world," Lauren continues, they are responsible for these catastrophic changes in weather.[16] There are earthquakes in California, tornadoes in the southern states, and hurricanes throughout the U.S. In addition to wild weather patterns and drought, the U.S. is riddled with disease and medical epidemics.

Lauren suffers excessively within this broken world in part because of her mother's neglect and symbolic abandonment. Lauren's mother took "Paracetco, the small pill, the Einstein power"[17] to sharpen her memory and thought processes, for two years prior to Lauren's birth. The result is that the daughter has a "hyperempathic" disease; she feels others' pain (and pleasure) so deeply that it can kill her. Several things are important to note here; the poisoned mother's body poisoned the daughter, and the mother died in childbirth. Within the context of the novel, the loss of the mother signifies, in part, the death of mother-earth. Yet, perhaps more importantly, the mother's drug addiction locates this violence as the *mother's* fault, hence the biological mother in the text is held responsible for the daughter's pain and subsequent abandonment.

The walled-in community is under constant threat because of the violence in the outside society. Lauren, unlike the other members of her neighborhood, fears they will not survive an attack from the outside looters, and she therefore makes plans for her future survival—reading books on log cabin building, native plant cultivation and soap making, and she prepares a backpack full of survival material. As Lauren predicts, her neighborhood is attacked and destroyed by thieves and murderers, and Lauren makes her escape, taking her prepared backpack and food from the symbolically fallen garden of her former neighborhood.

Lauren seeks a new, multicultural, interdependent vision of humanity, race, and nature. She leaves Los Angeles and its environs and journeys north, meeting with assorted people who eventually become members of Earthseed, Lauren's spiritual and utopian religion. People of all races and social backgrounds join this Earthseed group: "Black, White, Latino, Asian—and any mixture at all."[18] During this trek, Lauren meets her older lover Bankole, a medical doctor who has unscathed land in Humboldt County, California, with whom she bonds and plans the first of her Earthseed communities: Acorn. Even though the water is uncontaminated on Bankole's property, and the land has a substantial garden, this is not the final destination for Earthseed. "The Destiny of Earthseed is to take root among the stars" in living 'Heaven', Lauren says. If they do not escape the contaminated earth, they will become like the "smooth-skinned dinosaurs." They must go "Beyond Mars" to "Other star systems . . . and l]iving worlds."[19] In her utopian vision, then, they must plant new egalitarian societies, and "begin again and do things right this time." Merchant's earthly partnership ethic is impossible to achieve on this lapsarian earth for Lauren, thus she takes an approach of many explorers throughout history—including early European travelers who searched for Eden. Lauren and her Earthseed community will act as "colonists" who reclaim the lost paradise on other planets.[20] Paradoxically, when considering the racial and social implications of early European exploration and colonization—one of the first Earthseed ships to take flight at the end of *Talents* is named *The Christopher Columbus*. Given Lauren's status as a powerful black woman, such a provocatively imperialist title seems ironic for her utopian vision.

In the sequel, *The Parable of the Talents,* the daughter's voice functions as an external narrator that ties the mother's (Lauren's) journal entries together. As the journal entries begin in 2032, Laurens' dreams for Earthseed and Acorn take root, and she gives birth to her baby girl, Larkin. Global warming is on the rise, there are major landslides on the coast of California, the land is drying up, and the redwoods are dying. Bankole fears for their child, as the conservative, violent *Christian America* grows in power in the outside world—burning all those who are deemed "different" as witches. "A witch, in their view, tends to be a Moslem, a Jew, a Hindu, a Buddhist. . . .A witch may also be an atheist [or] a 'cultist'[,]" Lauren writes.[21] Bankole begs Lauren to give up Earthseed and put her role as mother first. "Now that you're a mother," he says, "you've got to let go of some of the Earthseed thinking and *think of your child.* I want you to look at Larkin and think of her every time you want to make some grand decision."[22] Yet Lauren will not relinquish her community of Acorn, despite the dangers that surround them. She says, "I'm no more likely to leave Acorn now than I am to leave Larkin."[23] Thus Lauren does not submit to "the ideals of intensive mothering", and instead attempts to balance her role as mother with her role as religious, environmental, and political leader; the result is that the baby Larkin is abducted by soldiers of the *Christian America* militia when the Acorn community is attacked and turned into a horrific internment camp. Larkin is placed with a *Christian America* family for adoption, as are all the Earthseed children, and Bankole dies. Later, after her escape, Lauren tries to find Larkin (who is renamed Asha Vere by her adopted parents), but she is unsuccessful. Near the end of *Talents*, when Larkin/Asha is an adult, mother and child reunite. But while Lauren wants, desperately, to reconnect with Larkin/Asha, the daughter cannot forgive the choices her mother has made.[24]

Lauren's decision to put her utopian community before her child's immediate safety makes Lauren a "dangerous," cultish, monster to Larkin/Asha. She is an "overwhelming" figure, according to the daughter, "who [wants] to get away from" Lauren when they finally meet. While Lauren's dream for Earthseed to "take root among the stars"[25] and create a "partnership with [the] environment[,]"[26] may come to fruition at the novel's close, as the first shuttles are launched, they do so without the participation of Larkin/Asha, as Lauren once hoped and dreamed. The daughter despises her mother and her vision for Earthseed—what Larkin/Asha tellingly calls Lauren's, "first 'child,' and in some ways her only 'child'."[27] Larkin ridicules her mother's dream and suggests that rather than traveling to other planets, work needs to be done to repair things "here on earth," where there are "so many diseases, [and there is] so much hunger, so much poverty, such suffering."[28] The counter-narrative of the daughter's angry voice thus undermines Lauren's potentially ecofeminist utopian vision and begs the following questions: Why not tend to earth first as Larkin/Asha suggests, rather than search for a "distant mythical paradise" somewhere else?[29] And, at whose expense are these new worlds to be built? What about the "frozen human and animal embryos" carried aboard the ships?[30] What living beings might be harmed by this potentially imperialistic, mechanistic, reproductive project?

While Larkin's implied questions are important to consider, we know that the earth's social and physical ecology may be past all hope for any kind of equitable partnership to take place between humans and nonhuman nature in *The Parables*. We also know there is a counter to Larkin's matriphobic narrative, as a form of communal parenting and an ethic of nurturing has taken place throughout *Sower* and *Talents*, within the community of Earthseed. Patricia Melzer argues that while Lauren herself is not a "conventional" mother, her utopian community offers a compassionate model of care for others that "can give meaning to life and can heal internal wounds." This model contrasts sharply with the alienation and social isolation found in the dominant culture. Although mothering is "fundamental" part of the Earthseed community, "Butler's concept of mothering rejects the white stereotypical ideal of the nurturing self-sacrificing mother within the partriarchal society. Instead, it embodies involvement and commitment to the community at large that in principle is independent of gender."[31] In *Sower*, for instance, Natividad breastfeeds her child at the same time as she nurses the baby of a dead woman, and men parent as well as women. Earthseed's ideology of mothering thus functions to "subvert" Larkin/Asha's narrative, as Clara Escoda Agusti suggests.[32] Indeed, a large part of the Earthseed project is the protection and nurturing of *all* lost children, of all races and all backgrounds. Shared parenting, and a de-emphasizing of the biologically-linked, nuclear family, is practiced, in this instance, to the service of the greater communal good, and this feeds into Lauren's larger Earthseed partnership ethic:

> Partnership is giving, taking
> learning, teaching, offering the
> greatest possible benefit while doing
> the least possible harm. Partnership
> is mutualistic symbiosis. Partnership
> is life.
> Any entity, any process that
> cannot or should not be resisted or
> avoided must somehow be
> partnered. Partner one another.
> Partner diverse communities. Partner
> life. Partner any world that is your
> home. Partner God. Only in
> partnership can we thrive, grow,
> Change. Only in partnership can we
> live.
> —Lauren Olamina from *The Earthseed Books*[33]

For Butler, partnership parenting or "othermothering," a multicultural ethic of care, and environmentalist partnership ethics are all intertwined and function symbiotically. This ecological and maternal partnership ethic opens a space for a liberating ecofeminist utopian vision of interdependent relations between humans and nonhuman nature. In Lauren's spiritual quest, "*Nature / Is all that exists. / It's the earth / And all that is on it / It's the universe / And all that's in it/ It's God, Never at rest . . .* [34] Thus, for Butler, nature is "everything and everywhere," just as the potential for a caring and equal partnership among all living creatures pervades the human capacity to unify and heal the chaotic dystopian world.

In *Into the Forest*, Hegland's dystopian portrait of a post-holocaust society takes place in the near future in Northern California. All technology and mail delivery have failed, and the two main characters, teenagers Nell and Eva, live alone after the deaths of their parents in a house in the woods thirty-two miles from the nearest town. This novel, like *The Parables,* critiques the damage the human race has done to the earth. Nell writes:

> We had been in an oil crisis for at least two generations. There were holes in the ozone, our forests were vanishing, our farmlands were demanding more and more fertilizers and pesticides to yield increasingly less—and more poisonous—food. There was an appalling unemployment rate, an overloaded welfare system, and people in the inner cities were seething with frustration, rage, and despair. Schoolchildren were shooting each other at recess. Teenagers were gunning down motorists on the freeways. Grown-ups were opening fire on strangers in fast-food restaurants.

Now they are surrounded by a world in full-fledged "ruin"; "an earthquake caused one of California's nuclear reactors to melt down, and the Mississippi River flooded . . . violently."[35] Military groups have bombed the Golden Gate Bridge, wars are being waged all over the world, the White House is burning. Now, "old rules are . . . suspended."[36] No civil order remains in society at large and the natural environment is in grave peril. Like Butler, therefore, Hegland links environmental degradation with sociopolitical conflict.

Into the Forest counters this dystopian social and environmental violence with the promotion of a partnership ethic with nature through the reconfiguring of the mother-nature bond. Nell's and Eva's mother is alienated from nature, and the novel suggests that this separation leads to the mother's death and the potential demise of her daughters. Certainly, the mother's relationship to nature runs counter to the ecological partnership ethic in the text. Hegland's novel in the end comes full circle, however, as a new model of communal parenting is put into effect and a reconnection with the mother in nature is found. The narrator, Nell, as well as her sister Eva, are (re)born through a regenerative, ecologically balanced, powerful connection between humans and nonhuman world.

As children, Nell and Eva, have been raised in isolation, home-schooled in the world of the idealized forest. This intense relationship to nature has been forged *against* their mother's will. When the girls are toddlers, they wander through the woods with their father. They looked at "wildflowers, listened to the birds, and splashed in the clear trickle of the creek. We picked up leaves and poked at centipedes and waterstriders while he towered above us."[37] The father is positioned as a benevolent "tree" as part of the forest he stands near as a guide and aid. In contrast, their mother, a former city dweller and ballerina, fears the wilderness and wants to keep her daughters separated from nature. At six and seven, the girls long to go by themselves into the forest. "Every flower and bird and mysterious crashing beckoned for us to clamber up through the trees and ferns, but our mother insisted that we keep to the road." The mother tells them, "'You are too young . . . You'll get lost. It's not safe.'" She fears they will be injured by "wild pigs," "rattlesnakes," "bears," and "wild plants."[38] Their father insists that the girls will be safe and they are allowed to enter the forest, *despite* their mother's opposition. The mother herself never leaves the house or domesticated garden, and she watches the girls play from behind the screen of a large picture window.

Significantly, when the mother contracts cancer, she plants a rim of red tulip bulbs around the edge of their property—marking a space between the family's domesticated yard and the wilderness. Later, while the mother is on her deathbed, the tulips come up and form a "ring of fire. . . a band of red that separated the tame green of [the] lawn from the wild green of the forest."[39] After the mother dies, the flowers bloom annually—a reminder of the separation between the mother's domesticated garden and the wilderness.

In the forest, free from their mother's fears, however, and with the encouragement of their father who believes it is in nature that the girls may obtain their best education, they create an imaginary world in harmony with nature. Nell writes:

> Ours is a mixed forest, predominantly fir and second-growth redwood but with a smattering of oak and madrone and maple. Father said that before it was logged our land had been covered with redwoods a thousand years old, but all that remained of that mythic place were a few fallen trunks the length and girth of beached whales and several charred stumps the size of small sheds.
>
> When we were about nine or ten, Eva and I discovered one of those stumps about a mile above our house and made it our own. It was hollow, and the space inside was large enough to serve as a fort, castle, teepee, and cottage. A tributary of the creek that borders our clearing ran near it and provided us with water for wading, washing, and mudpie making. We kept a chipped tea set up there along with blankets, dress-up clothes, and broken pans, and there we spent every minute we could steal or wheedle, playing Pretend.
>
> "Pretend" . . . one of us would say as soon as we reached the stump . . . we're Indians." *Or goddesses. Or orphans. Or witches.* "And pretend. . . that we're lost." *That we're stalking deer. That we're going to dance with the fairies. That a bear's coming to get us and we have to hide.*[40]

The forest is portrayed by Nell as an "idyllic" mythic paradise; the ancient stump is reminiscent of an idealized prelapsarian past, the old growth forest, before mankind destroyed the ancient tree. What is left is a beautiful place, hollowed out by time, in which the girls can explore being fairies, witches, feminized pan-like creatures—"wood nymphs." Like "Native Americans" they stalk deer, and interact in partnership with wild creatures. Non-human creatures cannot hurt them—they are untouched by bears, boars, and rattlesnakes and the forest contains "everything" they need.[41] As they grow into adolescence, however, Eva foregoes playing in the forest for her new interest in ballet, and eventually Nell gives in, leaves their natural heaven, and turns to her computer, her academic studies, and her preparations for Harvard.

In a sense, "injured nature" retaliates for what human beings have done to mother- earth—as both parents die from technological or mechanistic forces.

First their mother dies from cancer; the novel implies that the mother is killed by her exposure to the toxic dyes and mordents she used in coloring the yarns for her weavings. Later, their father is killed by his own chainsaw in the forest. After their parents' deaths, the sisters go through many months of mourning and they suffer a major crisis: A male invader searching for "gas" rapes Eva because she refuses to give up their small remaining supply. This event symbolically replicates much ecofeminist theory that links the rape of feminized earth (for oil in this case) with the rape of the female body. Eva suffers deeply as a result of the rape, and she becomes pregnant and nearly dies in childbirth. Nell saves Eva by bringing her sister back to their mythical tree stump in the forest, and it is there where the sisters are each reborn—as mothers in connection with the land.

At first things do not go so smoothly, for the sisters, however. Before the birth, Nell and Eva heal the wounds of rape through an incestuous love scene, and later Nell cares for and nurses Eva's baby Burl/Robert, as Eva is too sick to do so herself. But as Eva heals, she becomes resentful of the bond between Nell and Burl, and she insists that Nell stop nursing the baby. "He doesn't need two mothers," Eva says in a rage.[42] Nell runs off for a period of time, stops herself from lactating by drinking herbs, and when Nell returns to her sister, she resolves to forego her mothering relationship with the baby. At this point, Eva is forgiving and willing to share her child, and she says that Nell may nurse Burl. Ultimately, however, both sisters decide that neither can possess the baby; just as their mother used to tell them when they were children, Eva says Burl "is his own [person]."[43]

Nell discovers that it is in the tree stump, in the forest, in nature, that a reunification with the *earth and "the primordial Great mother"*[44] may be found, and a true healing between humans and nonhuman nature may take place. Near the close of the novel, while in the forest, Nell hears her "*Mother'[s]*" voice—with a capital M.[45] It turns out to be a female bear that comes to the stump and sleeps next to Nell:

> *I dreamed she [the bear] bore me from the hot mystery of her womb, squeezing me down the tunnel of herself, until I dropped, helpless and unresisting, to the earth. Blind and mewling, I scaled her huge body, rooting until the nipple filled my throat. Later, her tongue sought me out. Lick by insistent lick, she shaped the naked lump of me, molded my body and senses to fit the rough tug of her intention. Lick by Lick, she birthed me again, and when she was finished, she shambled on, left me—alone and Nell-shaped—in Her forest.*[46]

Nell's (re)birth through her symbolic dream-connection with the female bear-as-mother leads her to the realization that she must abandon the dystopian society of the post-apocalyptic world, reconnect with her family members, and live in nature. Nell convinces Eva that they have no chance of survival in what is left of society at large. The sisters then burn down their house with the last of the remaining gasoline, and they "enter the forest for good."[47]

The Parables and *Forest* demonstrate how patriarchal violence has denigrated nature and women's bodies, and Butler's and Hegland's protagonists seek havens outside of their hegemonic dystopian worlds in feminized Edens. Each of these novels explores the need to find a human "partnership ethic" with nature. For Hegland, we are all living in the "fugue" state Nell describes, exploiting nature and foolishly relying on electricity and oil/gas as infinite resources. This time of extreme environmental degradation and exploitation—created out of our need to support our late-capitalist dependency on nonrenewable resources—is only a brief period in human history, and it is time, as Lauren, Eva, and Nell suggest, for us to find a way to live in balance with nature. For Nell and Eva, this is accomplished by ending our dependency on wasteful, mechanistic, and destructive forms of technology. For Lauren Olamina, the future rests in the socially and racially conscious communal partnership relationship, in which a balance between technology, and nonhuman nature and humans may be found for all living beings—on other planets. As Merchant suggests, "a partnership ethic brings human beings and nonhuman nature into a dynamically-balanced, more nearly equal relationship with each other."[48] It is this partnership ethic that Lauren, Nell and Eva seek.

Notes

1. Karen J. Warren, "Taking Empirical Data Seriously: An Ecofeminist Philosophical Perspective," *Ecofeminism: Women, Culture, Nature* (Bloomington: Indiana University Press, 1997), 3.

2. Carolyn Merchant, *Reinventing Eden,: The Fate of Nature in Western Culture* (New York: Routledge Press, 2004), 226.

3. Merchant, 3.

4. Merchant, *Radical Ecology: The Search for a Livable World* (New York: Routledge, 2005), 83.

5. Merchant, 84.

6. Merchant, 85

7. Merchant, *Reinventing Eden*, 223.

8. Merchant, *Radical Ecology*, 196.

9. Andrea O'Reilly, *Rocking the Cradle: Thoughts on Motherhood, Feminism and the Possibility of Empowered Mothering* (Toronto: Demeter Press, 2006), 43.

10. "Community mothering and othermothering . . . emerged in response to black mothers' needs and served to empower black women and enrich lives," O'Reilly explains. It is a mode of collective transformation and political and social activism, in O'Reilly, 112–113. See, also, Patricia Hill Collins, who explains this mode of 'othermothing' in "The Meaning of Motherhood in Black Culture and Black Mother-Daughter Relationships," Patricia Bell-Scott and Beverley Guy-Sheftall, eds. *Double Stitch: Black Women Write About Mothers and Daughters* (New York: HarperPerennial Press, 1993), 42–60, and bell hooks, "Revolutionary Parenting." *Feminist Theory: From Margin to Center* (Boston: South End Press, 1990), 41–49.

11. For relevant criticism on the dystopia/utopia in *The Parables*, see Madhu Dubey, "Folk and Urban Communities in African-American Women's Fiction: Octavia Butler's Parable of the Sower," *Studies in American Fiction*, 27, (1999, Spring): 1, 103–28; Patricia Melzer, "'All That You Touch You Change': Utopian Desire and the Concept of Change in Octavia Butler's *Parable of the Sower* and *Parable of the Talents*," *Femspec*, 3 (2002): 2, 31–52; Peter B. Stillman, "Dystopian Critiques, Utopian Possibilities, and Human Purposes in Octavia Butler's 'Parables'," *Utopian Studies*, 14, (2003): 1, 15-35; Hazel Carby, "Figuring the Future in Los(t) Angeles," *Comparative American Studies*, 1 (2003):1, 19–34; Jim Miller, "Post-Apocalyptic Hoping: Octavia Butler's Dystopian Utopian Vision, Science Fiction Studies, 25 (1988): 2, 336–360. See also, Zaki Hoda, "Utopia, Dystopia, and Ideology in the Science Fiction of Octavia Butler," *Science Fiction Studies*, 17, (1990): 2, 239–251.

12. Stillman, "Dystopian Critiques," 15.

13. Miller, "Post-Apocalyptic Hoping," 349, 351.

14. Sylvia Mayer, "Genre and Environmentalism: Octavia Butler's Parable of the Sower, Speculative Fiction, and the African American Slave Narrative," Sylvia Mayer, ed., Res*toring the Connection to the Natural World: Essays on the African American Environmental Imagination* (Münster, Germany: LIT Press, 2003), 176.

15. Octavia E. Butler, *Parable of the Sower* (New York: Aspect Press, 1993), 17, 18.

16. Butler, 57.

17. Butler, 12.

18. Butler, *Parable of the Talents* (New York: Aspect, 1998), 47.

19. Butler, *Sower*, 222.

20. Butler, *Talents*, 394.

21. Butler, 20.

22. Butler, 195 (italics mine).

23. Butler, 194.

24. Melzer calls Lauren a rather "'un-motherly' figure in the conventional sense in that she rejects the passivity regarding public/political life associated with the role"41.

25. Butler, *Talents*, 442.

26. Butler, 442.

27. Butler, 443.

28. Butler, 416.

29. Butler, 419.

30. Butler, 422.

31. Melzer, "'All That You Touch You Change,' 41–42.

32. Clara Escoda, "The Relationship Between Community and Subjectivity in Octavia E. Butler's *Parable of the Sower*," *Extrapolation*, 46 (2005): 3,

33. Butler, *Talents*, 147.

34. Butler, 419.

35. Jean Hegland, *Into the Forest* (New York: Bantam Books Press, 1998), 10.

36. Hegland, 111.

37. Hegland, 50.

38. Hegland, 50–51.

39. Hegland, 47.

40. Hegland, 51 (italics mine).

41. Hegland,, 52.

42. Hegland,, 226.

43. Hegland, 231.
44. O'Reilly, *Rocking the Cradle,* 95.
45. Hegland, 229.
46. Hegland, 230.
47. Hegland, 241.
48. Merchant, *Radical Ecology*, 84.

8

Natural Resistance: Margaret Atwood as Ecofeminist or Apocalyptic Visionary

H. Louise Davis

In 1976 the journal *Signs* devoted two articles to Margaret Atwood's novel *Surfacing*. Feminist scholars Carol P. Christ and Judith Plaskow debated whether Margaret Atwood's novel *Surfacing* could be claimed as an ecofeminist text or one by a Canadian nationalist writer. In the same edition of *Signs*, Atwood herself responds to the debate by reiterating that her role is that of a writer, not of a social critic, and that her novel "is not a treatise at all, but a novel."[1] Despite her wish to be labeled as nothing other than a writer concerned with exploring what is "true about human nature,"[2] it comes as no surprise that ecofeminist scholars have attempted to claim Atwood's work as support for their own cause. Throughout her literary career, Atwood has continued to examine ecofeminist issues. She has written poetry, short fiction, and novels that both depict the "bonds between women and nature" and critique "their parallel oppressions and encouraging an ethic of caring and politics of solidarity,"[3] without resorting to essentialist formulations of either femininity or the natural world.

Many ecofeminists argue that it is imperative that women recognize the parallels between their oppression and that of the natural world, and that both women and nature should be conceived of and represented as agents in their own right. As a result of their extraordinary encounters with the natural world, almost all of Atwood's female protagonists go through a transformative stage in which they come to acknowledge both their connection to nature and their own agency. In contrast, however, nature is rarely depicted as anything other than a catalyst that prompts the psychical and physical metamorphoses of the women who explore or retreat into it. In this sense, many of Atwood's women appear to invade and use nature in the same ways that men invade and use women's bodies and, thus, nature can be read as the subordinate to womanhood in Atwood's work. On the other hand, as Atwood explains in "A Reply," her aim is to explore "human nature" and not, necessarily, to further any political goal.[4] In much of her work, Atwood chooses to focus upon the transformations of her characters as opposed to the changes that occur to and within their temporary environment. This does not imply, however, that either natural or cultural environments do not shift and change. The publication of her novel *Oryx and Crake* in 2003 marks a shift in Atwood's focus; whereas, in her earlier texts, she explores the effects of nature upon the human being, in *Oryx* she examines the consequences of humans' interactions with nature. Although Atwood continues to explore women's issues and human modes of representation and signification, ecological concerns are the primary focus of the text. *Oryx*, the most apparently apocalyptic of Atwood's works, becomes the most ecofeminist.

That said, this novel has received little attention from ecofeminists, many of whom appear more concerned with ecofeminist aspects of *Surfacing* than with any other of Atwood's texts. This is partially due to the fact that *Surfacing*, a story of a woman's quest into the wilderness, can easily be claimed by the ecofeminist movement; it holds all the ingredients of a complex ecofeminist novel in the sense that woman and nature are at once correlated and at odds with one another. In contrast, *Oryx and Crake*, along with the other texts examined in this paper, are not immediately recognizable as compatible with ecofeminist aims. Particularly *Oryx*, because it is a science-fiction novel that depicts a male protagonist, seems out of place within the (unofficial) ecofeminist canon. Before I demonstrate how *Oryx* expands both the definitions and scope of ecofeminism, however, it seems prudent to consider exactly what ecofeminists typically expect of the literary text, or, more specifically, of Atwood's work. Through an examination of the debates surrounding *Surfacing*, discussions of its contributions to ecofeminist aims and its failures as an ecofeminist text, I expose the limited definitions of ecofeminist writing offered by numerous critics. I thus provide a rationale that allows all of Atwood's works to be considered, if not radically ecofeminist, at least ecofeminist friendly.

Although *Surfacing* is the first of Atwood's novels to be labeled ecofeminist, the text is possibly the most contentious, in terms of the ecofeminist debate. This debate, about Atwood's commitment and contribution to the ecofeminist movement, born out of the Christ-Plaskow essays, still continues on into the twenty-first century. Most commentary surrounds Atwood's portrayal of the narrator as a woman who, upon realizing her complicity in the destruction of natural artifacts (including her own unborn child), sheds all the symbols of civilization and retreats into the wilderness.

It is the narrator's encounter with the heron that signals the beginning of her first quest into the depths of the wilderness and into the depths of her own desire. Upon seeing the dead bird suspended from the tree, she starts to question the desire to control or kill; a desire that, according to many scholars who have written on *Surfacing*, she has shared up until this point. The bird, in being representative of both those who kill and those who are killed, forces the narrator not only to accept her own complicity, but also to reconsider her own desire.

> It was behind me, I smelled it before I saw it; then I heard the flies. The smell was like decaying fish. I turned around and it was hanging upside down by a thin blue nylon rope tied round its feet and looped over a tree branch, its wings fallen open. It looked at me with its mashed eye. . . I wondered what part of them the heron was, that they needed so much to kill it.[5]

Here the narrator is confronted with an image that bridges the gap between life and death, nature and civilization. Through its death, those that killed the heron can alleviate their own fear of death. Once tied to the tree, the heron becomes a spectacle; it is a ritualistic sign of man's power over nature. The smell, sound, and sight of the dead heron forces the narrator to realize how she, in not being unlike the heron in the minds of the killers, also functions as a spectacle that alleviates men's fears of castration and death. When the bird returns her look, with its one mashed eye, she is forced to "apprehend [her] own specularity."[6] No longer is she able to uphold the illusion that she controls the gaze. This leads to her sense of powerlessness, but also reinforces her sense of complicity as, in attempting to fit in to the civilized world, she has supported both the illusion and the dominance of the male gaze.

Her retreat into nature, her need to escape the trappings of patriarchal civilization, is evidence that she refuses to accept her positioning as specularized object of desire. Although, as Sally Robinson astutely suggests, "Atwood does not create a viable space from which her protagonist can speak her desire,"[7] she at least experiences this desire, and it is this experience that provides hope for her at the end of the novel. Through the narrator's encounter with the heron, Atwood demonstrates how women and nature are both objectified and negated through processes of representation. Throughout her work, Atwood employs equations of women and nature to expose the mechanisms of patriarchal systems of representation and signification that objectify and negate women and the natural world in similar ways.

In *Undomesicated Ground*, Stacy Alaimo supports the notion that the visual colonization of the female body is parallel to that of natural artifacts within the text. In her discussion of David's attempt to persuade Anna to "get naked" for the camera, a shot that will parallel the shots of the dead bird, Alaimo states "side by side, the heron and the naked lady become objects for the male gaze."[8] Here Alaimo acknowledges how Atwood's novel challenges the domination of the male gaze. However, in her critical analysis of *Surfacing*, she tends to ignore the benefits to the ecofeminist movement of fictional texts that unsettle the cultural systems by which women and nature are oppressed. Her argument, that the "alliance that the novel has forged between nature and women manifests itself as a narrative that underwrites heterosexuality and condemns reproductive freedom,"[9] is somewhat problematic because it is based upon the notion that Margaret Atwood's ideological and ecological stance is the same as that of her narrator. Although it is true to say that the narrator views nature in a problematic way, it is wrong to assume that Atwood views the nature of womanhood similarly. As Atwood clearly states in "A Reply," her novel "concerns characters with certain backgrounds and habits of mind, placed in a particular environment and reacting to it in their own ways."[10]

As Carol P. Christ suggests, the narrator's view of the nature/woman connection is based upon essentialist assumptions. Christ states:

> The experience of nature as great power, the content of Atwood's protagonist's religious vision, seems to reflect a female standpoint in the modern West, because the biological experiences of women in menstruation, pregnancy, childbirth, and nursing often enable women to retain a sense of closeness to nature, which men tend to lose in urbanized culture.[11]

As various ecofeminists have demonstrated, this type of equation of nature with female biology simply serves to justify the patriarchal domination of both.[12] As I have demonstrated, unlike her narrator, Atwood's equation of women and nature is based upon their parallel positions as Other, and not upon biological determinism. Whereas her narrator confuses the ecofeminist cause through her essentialist views of nature, Atwood furthers it through exposing those socio-cultural mechanisms by which both women and nature are subordinated.

Unlike Alaimo, Sally Robinson distinguishes between the aims of Atwood and those of her narrator. Robinson's critique of *Surfacing* is based upon the form, rather than upon the content of the novel. While recognizing its strengths, Robinson argues that Atwood's exploration of "feminine territory" and "feminine language" is limited by her use of "conventional narrative patterns" and techniques.[13] Robinson's argument proves more convincing than Alaimo's because Robinson approaches the text from a feminist literary angle, and not from a more prescriptive ecofeminist angle. She does not negate Atwood's aims, but her methods.

In her "Circle/Mud Poems," published two years after the publication of *Surfacing* (and fourteen years prior to Robinson's article), Atwood returns to the themes and images that preoccupy *Surfacing*. However, her treatment of these themes differs greatly as, in her poetry, she employs the types of disruptive and disorientating narrative techniques that Robinson, an advocate of *écriture feminine*, would commend. Despite Atwood's innovative explorations of women and nature in poetry and short experimental fictions, few feminist or ecofeminist critics (including Robinson) have paid them any attention. Contrasting such works with *Surfacing* proves to be a fruitful exercise for any critic with an interest in ecofeminism. As Atwood rarely depicts the nature/culture dichotomy or the nature/woman parallel in exactly the same way twice, comparative analyses of her fictional work provide the ecofeminist with multiple models with which to approach and conceive of feminist and environmentalist issues.

Throughout the "Circle/Mud Poems" Atwood uses ambiguity, accusation, and a blurring of human and animal boundaries to emphasize the subordination of the natural world and, by association, femininity. In the fifth untitled poem in

"Circle/Mud Poems" (1974), she presents a message about human (inter)actions within the natural world similar to that presented in *Surfacing*. However, the form that this message takes is distinctly different.

The poem opens with a statement of deliberate passivity; the poetic voice states "I made no choice / I decided nothing."[14] Unhindered by the restraints of punctuation, floating alone at the top of the page, this statement first appears to be a vague passing thought, an admission of innocence that needs no further elaboration or clarification. However, when placed in the context provided by the rest of the poem, the "vacant" statement proves not to be "innocent" but rather insidious. Passivity is rendered as complicity as the poetic voice explains that, to decide nothing is still to make a decision, and that decisions have consequences. Exactly whom it is that makes the decisions, whom it is that complies with them, and whom they affect, is never revealed.

In addition, the poetic voice never reveals its identity and, thus, the reader is left to ponder who "I" may be. Similarly the "you" to whom the poem is addressed, also remains a mystery. This refusal to identify "you" or "I" leads to an ambiguity that is both intriguing and discomforting. It is quite conceivable the "you" and "I" are one in the same; that "I" who "made no choice" and "decided nothing," is the same as "you" who "made the right choice" and that thought "of nothing."

Exactly what "you" and "I" have done, through deciding nothing, is explained in the second stanza of the poem, when the poetic voice makes reference to the arrival of "you," the intruder:

> One day you simply appeared in your stupid boat,
> your killer's hands, your disjointed body, jagged
> as a shipwreck,
> skinny-ribbed, blue-eyed, scorched, thirsty, the usual,
> pretending to be – what? a survivor?[15]

Any reader familiar with *Surfacing* is likely to make connections to the novel, particularly as the narrator arrives in the wilderness by boat. The image of the heron is evoked by the reference to "disjointed body," "skinny" ribs, and "blue" eyes. The ribs of the heron become visible when it is suspended, with its wings spread wide. Their thinness is further indication that they would be a meager source of food, that the heron was not killed so that the killer could eat or "survive". The blueness of the eyes is indicative, again, of the bird whose feathers are blue, whose eye stares at "you." However, as the use of the possessive pronoun "your" indicates, the poetic voice is not describing the murdered heron, but the one that murdered it. It is the one who possesses the "killer's hands" whose body is "disjointed" and "jagged," whose ribs are "skinny" and eyes are blue. The killer is the one who has entered nature to begin a quest, to "pretend" to survive in the wilderness. But, while surviving, the survivor has felt the need to kill and, in doing so, becomes like the one killed. In performing such a thoughtless act (as the voice states, "you think of nothing") the killer is also damaged, shipwrecked.[16] In presenting a killer who is in the boat, but is also shipwrecked, Atwood's poetic voice implies that all killers are victims in some way. This conflation of the killer/victim is, again, reminiscent of *Surfacing* and the narrator's comprehension of her own participation in her own victim-hood and the death of her unborn child.

Like Atwood's novel, the poem blurs images of killer and killed, predator and prey, human and nature/woman: it is neither possible nor desirable to separate them. In blurring traditional dichotomies between dominant and subordinate, in refusing to distinguish between the passively complicit "I" and the not innocent "you," Atwood's poem presents a message similar to that of the narrator in *Surfacing*. However, in presenting the message in such an ambiguous and accusatory manner, she implicates the reader in a way that no novel can. The "you" that the poetic voice accuses is also the "I" who reads. Such a technique is invaluable to the ecofeminist cause because it raises readers' awareness of their own participation in oppressive systems of signification and representation.

Like the poem, Atwood's short story "The Bog Man," is filled with ambiguities. These ambiguities arise from the fact that the story is constantly in a state of revision. As the reader is well aware of these revisions, she/he is never quite able to ascertain whether the version she/he is reading is at all accurate, or if it is "dubious," "more or less on the edge" of the truth, "sort of within striking distance" of what actually happened.[17]

"The Bog Man" opens with the claim that "Julie broke up with Connor in the middle of a swamp."[18] Despite the decisiveness and clarity of this statement, the narrator soon reveals that events cannot be summarized so succinctly, that the statement needs clarification. In fact, the statement is a revised version of itself. Julie constantly and "silently revises," to the point that her story eventually becomes "like an artifact from a vanished civilization," Connor becomes "almost an anecdote, and Julie. . . almost old."[19]

Throughout the text, Julie is concerned with edges and boundaries, not because she wishes to cross them, but because she is losing the ability to perceive them. Before their arrival in mainland Scotland to search for the bog man, Julie and Connor spend their time visiting "sites of human sacrifice" in the Orkney Islands.[20] There "the fields were green, the sun shone" and Julie felt a mysterious connection to the standing stones. In contrast, when on the mainland of Northern Scotland, Julie is confined to a dark room in an unfamiliar, semi-civilized town. In such a space, she finds it difficult to perceive of her situation clearly.

Julie's thoughts consistently lose their form as she "silently" revises and re-revises her relationship with her married lover, Connor. Her revisions are an attempt to deal with the anxiety that her affair, within its new context, causes her. However, the more she re-views and re-evaluates, the more anxious she becomes. Connor's wife, who posed no threat to her at the onset of the affair, becomes "more solid" as time goes on: "this invisible wife has put on flesh, has gradually acquired solidity and presence."[21] In contrast, Julie has started to lose all definition. As time goes on, Julie risks becoming invisible as she desolidifies. She is no longer able to identify her own edges because, in the room where she spends most of her time, the light is poor (dulled by the grubby white curtains that cover the windows) and her mirror is nothing more than a piece of "wavering patchy glass."[22] She can no longer determine her features through her interactions with Connor (as his Other, as distinct from him) because they mostly occur in the dark or at a distance. She rarely sees him, except in the pub or the pouring rain and "[h]e does not need to see her, she has been seen enough" by him, she thinks, in the early stages of their relationship.[23]

As a result of her failing relationship and her inhospitable environment, Julie is undergoing a process of absorption or dilution. According to June Deery, it is not unusual for Atwood's characters to be diffuse or suffer from their diffusion. She states: "women's tendency to intermingle and be diffuse is not an advantage but indicates a lack of power."[24] Unlike the narrator in *Surfacing*, Julie does not wish to embrace her fluid, boundless state.

In her reaction to the bog man, Julie both asserts her belief in boundaries and offers a clue as to why hers are disintegrating. She feels "Surely there should be boundaries set upon the wish to know, on knowledge for its own sake."[25] Since the start of her relationship with Connor, Julie has undergone a series of excavations and examinations by Connor, similar to those he performs on his sacrificial sites and sacrificial artifacts. At the beginning of their relationship Connor took Julie's body "seriously," he insisted upon the lights being on during sex; he insisted upon examining her closely. Her response was to "worship" him, participate in his "radiance" and bask in his "light"; "she had been possessed by some notion of self-sacrifice."[26] However, as she stares at the bog man, a figure that has undergone a real sacrifice, she no longer wishes to occupy his position.

For Julie, the bog man's sacrifice occurs, not when he dies by the hands of the archaic "nature goddesses," but when he is exhumed by archeologists. She sees his "digging-up, this unearthing of him, as a desecration,"[27] perhaps because she identifies with him. Like her, his edges have become diffuse. Like him, she is "almost" ancient.

In one of the few published analyses of the short story, "Strangers With Gates: Margaret Atwood's *Wilderness Tips*," Carol L. Beran links, not Julie, but Connor to the bog man when she states that, at the story's end, "Connor and the bog man have great power and energy, now lost."[28] This loss of energy, Beran argues, is the result of Julie's constant revisions of the story that, in slowly reducing the significance of both Connor and the bog man each time it is told, results in their loss of definition. As I have argued, Julie and the bog man share similar fates. In equating the bog man with Connor, Beran also inadvertently equates Connor with Julie. Both lose solidity, both become more diffuse as the story progresses. However, whereas Julie's losses occur in the past, when she and Connor were in Scotland; Connor's diffusion occurs in the present, as Julie tells the story of their travels. In sharing similar characteristics, even if at different times, Julie and Connor become interchangeable. As a result, as Beran demonstrates, it becomes impossible to attribute moral blame to either one of them: "Are we to feel outrage at the professor for beginning an affair with a student without mentioning that he is married? Do we feel it is appropriate that Julie takes revenge on him as he declares his love for her?"[29]

Here Beran implies that Atwood makes it difficult to determine the difference between victim and victimizer in the story as both are one in the same. This blending of the culpable with the innocent is a motif that reoccurs in all the texts discussed. In addition, as in *Surfacing* and in the fifth poem of the "Circle/Mud Poems," the boundaries between nature and civilization are also blurred in "The Bog Man."

While in the bog, the bog man has been altered by tannic acid. He has assumed the characteristics of the land that preserved him. He has been claimed by the land and his borders are diffused by the land. The bog has similarly claimed other ancient symbols of civilization, as Julie notes, "the road that is so old . . . has cut itself into the land like a rut."[30] In the same way that civilization invades nature (by literally cutting into the land with shovels), the natural world overflows into the realm of civilization. Julie's immediate reaction is to retreat back into the civilized world, but this is not possible. Julie cannot escape from the bog: "Julie hunches up under the mound of damp coverings and tries without success to go to sleep. When at last she manages it, she dreams of the bog man, climbing in through her window, a dark tender shape, a shape of baffled longing, slippery with rain."[31]

Like the light that seeps under her door, the bog seeps into her room. In permeating her dreams, the bog man becomes a metaphor for Julie's unrepresentable desires. His "dark tender shape" and "baffled longing" evoke a sense of the archaic. He is a boundless, abject figure that exists within the realms of fantasy and reality, within the past and the present. He both appeals to, and repulses, Julie.

In many of Atwood's fictional texts the boundaries between nature and civilization are porous. Nature flows into civilization in the form of metaphor and feminine desire. Civilization invades and is superimposed over nature every time humans interact with and within the natural world. In *Oryx and Crake*, however, nature and civilization do not flow or cut into one another because, in effect, they are completely indistinguishable. Neither exist.

Arguably, it is Atwood's tendency toward abstraction, her implication that nature and culture are no longer separable even on a theoretical level, which makes the novel less appealing to critics concerned with ecofeminist debates. Abstractions tend to obscure definitions and, thus, inhibit political calls to action. However, I would argue that the diffusion of boundaries allows Atwood to avoid essentializing nature or culture—a criticism lodged at her by critics of *Surfacing*—while still furthering, somewhat unconventionally, the ecofeminist cause.

Jimmy, the novel's protagonist, struggles to survive within a scientifically oriented world. Unlike his father, or his friend Crake, Jimmy has little ability when it comes to science. His talents lie in words. When he graduates from high school with "underwhelming math marks," he is relegated to the Martha Graham Academy, a dilapidated liberal arts school on the edge of the Pleeblands. Despite his dissatisfaction, Jimmy does not attempt to leave the compound and escape into the wild world of the "Pleeblands": he has no desire to face the same fate as his mother, who escaped from her mundane family life only to become a fugitive, eventually executed for treason. Thus, he retreats into a fantasy world of word play and illicit sex.

Jimmy is a man in crisis. Even before all other human life is destroyed by Crake, Jimmy experiences anxiety over the breakdown of arbitrary yet well established boundaries by which he defines himself and the world around him. As the discussion between Jimmy and Crake in Watson-Crick lab indicates, there are no longer any absolutes in this world of wolvogs and ChickieNobs. It isn't even possible for Jimmy to determine "what is real."

> "How do those things work?" asked Jimmy, trying not to sound impressed.
> "Search me," said Crake. "I'm not in NeoGeologicals."
> "So, are the butterflies--are they recent?" Jimmy asked after a while. . . .
> "You mean did they occur in nature or were they created at the hand of man? In other words, are they real or fake?"
> "Mm," said Jimmy. He didn't want to get into the what is real thing with Crake.
> "You know when people get their hair dyed or their teeth done? Or women get their tits enlarged?"
> "Yeah?"
> "After it happens, that's what they look like in real time. The process is no longer important."[32]

Despite his talent with words, Jimmy does not posses the necessary vocabulary to express himself within a scientific community. He hesitates before asking Crake any questions, not merely to hide his admiration for Crake's work. Jimmy's modes of meaning rely upon the logic of dichotomies: for him word-signs can only make sense when they are defined in terms of their oppositions. Crake's scientifically advanced world no longer relies upon such oppositional logic. Within his environment, the lines that separate the natural from the artificial are no longer necessary or visible. Crake is simply concerned with progression, not in origins. He even erases his own origins, not only by disposing of his mother and step-father in the most gruesome ways, but by taking the name of an extinct bird for his own.

The only line of distinction that Jimmy can draw in Crake's environment is based upon time. His only certainty is that some aspects of nature existed prior to the advent of genetic engineering, and that others could not exist were it not for genetic engineering. Thus, when he asks about the butterfly, he chooses to couch his question in temporal terms. He asks "are they recent?" Crake, uninterested in semantics and unwilling to acknowledge the validity of any dichotomy, interprets the question correctly and, in doing so, illustrates the ridiculous nature of Jimmy's inquiries. When he asks whether Jimmy means are the butterflies "real or are they fake," he mocks Jimmy by revealing the flaws in his "archaic" logic: "natural" and "unnatural" are no longer useful categories in Crake's world.

As his "doctrine of unintended consequences" demonstrates, Crake's virtual obsession with "real time" allows him to ignore the processes of creation and life and focus purely on the finished product. Here he shows a blatant disregard for nature. In using women's beauty products as an example to prove his point that only "real time" matters, he betrays a similar disregard for women. Like nature, women function as commodities to be enhanced and manipulated in much the same way as the butterflies. Seemingly, Atwood's paralleling of nature and women here is as much a critique of the masculinization of science as it is of Crake's arrogance. In "Survival in Margaret Atwood's Novel *Oryx and Crake*," Earl G. Ingersoll describes how Atwood reveals the gendering of science and the arts through her depiction of relationships such as Jimmy's and Crake's. He states: "Jimmy and his defense of 'the arts' are positioned as 'feminine' and self-indulgent, while Crake and science are gendered 'masculine,' in a blatant masculinist performance of power."[33]

Here Ingersoll indicates that, even a world where boundaries are consistently blurred and the natural/artificial dichotomy is meaningless, gender divisions still exist. Atwood's text implies that to live in a civilized world is to live in a gendered world, that civilization almost always means the subordination of the feminine, that civilization is inherently patriarchal.

Posited as feminine, it is no surprise that language fails Jimmy. In this sense, he is not unlike the female protagonists in most of Atwood's fiction texts. However, unlike Julie in "The Bog Man," Jimmy has not yet learnt any linguistic techniques that might allow him to express his ideas through the slippages and gaps within language. In an attempt to find new modes of expression, and to re-establish his masculinity, Jimmy turns to self-help books from the Twentieth Century. "He compiled lists of old words too—words of a precision and suggestiveness that no longer had a meaningful application in today's world . . . He'd developed a strangely tender feeling towards such words, as if they were children abandoned in the woods and it was his duty to rescue them."[34]

This scene not only foreshadows future events, when Jimmy will rescue the children of Crake from the wilderness, but it also hints toward Jimmy's feelings of isolation and alienation. Jimmy is anxious that his language is being diluted, and that, soon, he will be unable to make any sense of the culture in which he lives. In re-animating the archaic and obscure words, he attempts to re-evoke, at least temporarily, a golden past where words, and men of words, had value. He assumes the role of protector of words, and rescuer of culture; a role that he will play on a larger scale after Crake destroys civilization.

In a sense, both Jimmy's interest in self-help texts, and his immersion in the wilderness after civilization fails, positions him as a Wild Man. In "Wet, Dark, and Low, Eco-Man Evolves from Eco-Woman," Andrew Ross explains the male desire to reclaim "an energy that has been sapped out by popular culture" through an invocation of the "pre-Greek myths of the Wild Man" as a response to ecofeminism.[35] He describes the twentieth Century "Wild Man Movement" as one that is fueled by self-help texts and designed to undermine the essentialist notion that women are closest to nature. Ross states that: "The market is composed primarily of heterosexual men in trouble, men who are alienated from work, romance, family, mainstream politics, and in search of some "truth" about themselves."[36]

Although Jimmy is not revolting against ecofeminism, he turns to self-help texts for the same reasons as Ross' Eco-men; that is, in an attempt to alleviate the anxiety that results from the dissolution of boundaries that radical sociocultural movements, such as ecofeminism, attempt to precipitate. Unlike the Eco-men, Jimmy's entrance into the wilderness is forced (he is an unwilling Wild Man) and not the result of a crisis of masculinity. And yet, prior to Crake's man-made disaster, Jimmy is in crisis. In the wild, he proves his masculinity and thus reclaims that dominant position for himself. Inadvertently, he also proves what Ross' Eco-men set out to prove: that men are as connected to nature as women. The difference between Jimmy and the Eco-men and women described by Ross and in other fictional texts by Atwood is that, for Jimmy, nature is threatening.

Within Crake's "Brave New World" Jimmy is the only symbol of the past, and the only hope for the return of civilization in the future. At the end of the novel, the reader is left to wonder if Snowman (Jimmy alters his name to suit his altered environment) will die from the virulent strand of genetically engineered bacteria that attack him through the cut in his foot, or if he will join the band of humans that have recently invaded his territory. If Jimmy and the other humans (two men and a woman) re-establish civilization, will they also re-establish the same male/female, civilization/nature dichotomies that led to the world's destruction in the first place? It seems that they just might. Snowman, a male, is the only one who knows the truth about the creation of the new world. In possessing such knowledge, and an ability to manipulate the "old" language for his own purposes, Snowman also possesses the most power. He functions like a God for the Children of Crake (who burn effigies of him when he is away for too long). In his role as God-like figure, and as a result of his remarkable Whiteness (hence the appellation Snowman), Snowman is reminiscent of the white settlers that entered the American wilderness to bring "civilization" to the supposedly ignorant natives.

In evoking the image of earlier colonists through her protagonist, Atwood implies that Snowman has the ability to re-establish a civilization in which the same mistakes will be repeated as femininity and nature will be, once again, positioned as nothing more than a subordinated resource to be used and improved upon. However, as with most of Atwood's fiction texts, the end of the novel is open-ended and ambiguous. As unwilling Wild Man and potential colonist, Snowman also blurs the boundaries between feminine and masculine, nature and civilization, victim and victimizer. He proves that women and nature are not inherently connected any more than men and nature; he acts as a bridge between the natural and the civilized worlds; he is both complicit in, and a casualty of the breakdown of boundaries that led to the advent of a "Brave New World." Thus, he becomes like Atwood's female protagonists. Like the narrator in *Surfacing*, the poetic voice in the fifth of her "Circle/Mud Poems," and Julie in the "Bog Man," he is faced with dilemmas, but also with choices.

Through her dissolution of boundaries, and in her exposure of the patriarchal systems of signification and representation that subordinate women and nature, Margaret Atwood furthers feminist aims. In doing so, she also aids the ecofeminist movement, yet not in a prescriptive or essentialist manner. This is no where so evident as in *Oryx and Crake*. Through the act of writing this novel, as science fiction text, Atwood finds both the imagery and the language with which to enter debates upon the ethicality of genetic research and manipulations and modifications of nature. Still, in referring to issues of body modification that pertain to women (as with the real tits reference in the passage quoted) and in acknowledging women's desire for RejoovenEsence products, she continues, in *Oryx*, to question the social expectations resultant from Western 'beauty regimes' that restrict and oppress women. Similarly, she deals with the notion of body image and reproduction throughout this text.

Wrapped up within debates of the 'natural' are, for Atwood, issues that concern women in their everyday lives. Arguably, Atwood demonstrates how reconfiguring notions of nature, and entering into the ecological and ethical debate that *Oryx* precipitates, is directly related to raising feminist issues about the status of women in present and future societies.

Through her male protagonist, Jimmy/Snowman, Atwood is able to explore environmental and ecological issues without focusing—but still considering—the complexities of female desire and representation. As she herself implies, her work and ideas are not static; like the scientific experiments she examines, they appear infinitely expansive. She demonstrates that there are a multitude of ways to contribute to the ecofeminist cause, without limiting one's creativity or scope.

In *Oryx*, Atwood extends the plausible—the inevitable—of scientific advancement to its logical conclusions. In exposing the logic of unintended consequences, she forces the reader (like the reader of *Circle/Mud Poems*) to become aware of her complicity in a world of scientific manipulation. It is this exposure, this implication of the reader, that again makes *Oryx* an invaluable contribution to the ecofeminist cause. Perhaps after reading the novel, readers will start to question what synthetics lurk within their KFC chicken breast meal, or what the long-term effects of their pharmaceutical enhancements might be! Such questioning is itself an antidote to "doing nothing," to Crake's doctrine of "unintended consequences," and can and often does lead to more organized consumer based activism. Ecofeminism should not simply be about defining or detailing the parallel oppressions of women and nature! Ecofeminism should also aim to provide the reader of both theory and fiction with the language and the tools necessary to effectively perceive and question those patriarchal structures that recklessly limit, oppress, and violate both human beings and their natural/cultural environments.

Oryx and Crake achieves this aim, allowing Atwood to enter into a dialogue about the plight of women, men, and the environment. Considering the popularity of Atwood's fiction, the size and varied nature of her audience, and the prominence of Atwood herself as a public figure, one could assume that her involvement in such a "dialogue" could help to precipitate a shift in common attitudes toward women and the environment.[37] However, when reading Atwood's fiction, one must remember, first and foremost, that her texts are stories and, as she herself states, "storytelling is a human activity and [is] valuable in its own right."[38]

Notes

1. Margaret Atwood. "A Reply," *Sign: Journal of Women in Culture and Society* 2, no. 2 (1976): 340– 341.

2. Katie Struckel, "The Human Nature of Margaret Atwood," *Reader's Digest* 80, no. 10 (2000): 35.

3. Stacy Alaimo, "Cyborg and Ecofeminist Interventions: Challenges for an Environmental Feminism," *Feminist Studies* 20, no. 1 (1994): 133.

4. Atwood. 340.

5. Margaret Atwood, *Surfacing* (London: Virago, 1979), 109. 113.

6. See Kaja Silverman, *The Threshold of the Visible World* (New York : Routledge, 1996), 165, for her revised reading of Sartre's notion of specularity.

7. Sally Robinson, "The 'Anti-Logos Weapon': Multiplicity in Women's Texts," *Contemporary Literature* 29, no. 1 (1988): 113.

8. Stacy Alaimo, *Undomesticated Ground: Recasting Nature as Feminist Space* (Ithaca NY: Cornell University Press, 2000), 141.

9. Alaimo, 142.

10. Atwood. "A Reply," 340.

11. Carol P. Christ, "Margaret Atwood: The Surfacing of Women's Spiritual Quest and Vision," *Sign: Journal of Women in Culture and Society* 2, no. 2 (1976): 326.

12. See both Stacy Alaimo, "Cyborg and Ecofeminist Interventions: Challenges for an Environmental Feminism," *Feminist Studies* 20, no. 1 (1994): 133- 152, and Mark Somma and Sue Tolleson-Rinehart, "Tracking the Elusive Green: Sex, Environmentalism, and Feminism in the United States and Europe," *Political Research Quarterly* 50, no. 1 (1997), 153- 169, for more information on essentialism within ecofeminism.

13. Sally Robinson, "The 'Anti-Logos Weapon',"115.

14. Margaret Atwood, *Eating Fire: Selected Poetry 1965–1995* (London: Virago, 1998): 160.

15. Atwood, 160.

16. The notions of 'boat' and 'shipwrecked' are again evocative of *Surfacing*, in which the 'Americans' deliberately kill the loons with their boat propellers—in the poem they ironically become shipwrecked.

17. Margaret Atwood, *Wilderness Tips*, 3rd ed. (London: Virago, 1997), 87.

18. Atwood, 87.

19. Atwood, 106.

20. Atwood, 92.

21. Atwood, 93.

22. Atwood, 99.

23. Atwood, 100.

24. June Deery, "Science for Feminists: Margaret Atwood's Body of Knowledge," *Twentieth Century Literature* 43, no. 4 (1994): 475.

25. Atwood, *Wilderness Tips,* 96.

26. Atwood, 90.

27. Atwood, 96.

28. Carol L. Beran, "Strangers within the Gates: Margaret Atwood's *Wilderness Tips*," in *Margaret Atwood's Textual Assassinations*. ed. Sharon Rose Wilson (Columbus OH: The Ohio University State Press, 2003), 79.

29. Beran, 79.

30. Atwood, *Wilderness Tips* 95.

31. Atwood, 99

32. Margaret Atwood, *Oryx and Crake*, (London: Virago, 2004): 235.

33. Earl E. Ingersoll. "Survival in Margaret Atwood's Novel *Oryx and Crake*," *Extrapolation* 45, no. 2 (2004): 167.

34. Atwood, *Oryx and Crake*, 230.

35. Andrew Ross, "Wet, Dark, and Low, Eco-Man Evolves from Eco-Woman," *Boundary* 2, 19, no. 2 (1992): 212.

36. Ross, 211.

37. Not only has Atwood authored numerous prize winning best-sellers, many of which are taught in schools throughout the world, but she has recently written for *Playboy*, many of her novels have been dramatized, and in 2003 a series entitled *The Atwood Stories* brought a selection of her short stories to the small screen.

38. Atwood, "A Reply," 340.

9

Touching the Earth: Gloria Anzaldúa and the Tenets of Ecofeminism

Allison Steele

Gloria Anzaldúa begins her book *Borderlands/ La Frontera* discussing culture and its affect on identity. She notes very succinctly that "culture forms our beliefs."[1] While this observation in itself may come as no surprise, she clarifies her use of the word "culture" to mean male-dominated Azteca-Mexica culture and articulates that current belief systems and identities are based largely on a patriarchal system of mythmaking which drove out female deities and female power and sent them underground.[2] Having been buried within the earth, it makes sense that Anzaldúa would see the rewriting of those myths not only to come from those within her Chicana heritage but also to come from those in touch with the earth. In fact, blatantly disavowing patriarchal myths and opening space for new myths, Anzaldúa argues the following:

> I am cultureless because, as a feminist, I challenge the collective cultural/religious male-derived beliefs of Indo-Hispanics and Anglos; yet I am cultured because I am participating in the creation of yet another culture, a new story to explain the world and our participation in it, a new value system with images and symbols that connect us to each other and to the planet.[3]

Despite what seems here to be a call to condemn men, that is not Anzaldúa's claim at all. Although she does denounce patriarchal myths, she does not denounce men. In fact, she sees women as complicit in maintaining dominant myths.[4] What she is calling for, instead, is for women (particularly Chicana women here, who have a history of politically controlled relationships with the land) to take some of that mythmaking back into their own hands—to write both women and the earth back into those stories.

Concerning those myths, when speaking with Inés Hernández-Ávila in 1991 about the oppressive Chicano patriarchal myth of the sun (a masculine entity) impregnating the earth (a feminine entity), Anzaldúa replied:

> Back to what you said in the beginning, about the sun impregnating the Earth. To me that's like the male impregnating the woman and one of the things I've seen—especially in the eco-feminist movement—has been women healing the Earth. So I'd like to see, with this sixth world sun, a new Woman-to-woman impregnation, rather than male to female, because we, the women, have been taking care of the Earth.[5]

Interestingly, although Anzaldúa recognizes the ecofeminist movement as well as advocates for the empowering connection between women and the Earth that is a tenet of ecofeminism, no critic, as yet, has explored the specific ways in which Anzaldúa herself might also contribute to that movement.[6] My contention is that Anzaldúa's identification of Chicanas/os and "border people" with the Earth and her call for a re-vision of patriarchal myths, such as the one previously mentioned, demonstrate the validity of such a connection. In *Borderlands/ La Frontera: The New Mestiza* (1987), and in several interviews in *Interviews/Entrevistas* (2000), Anzaldúa not only effectively responds to critiques of social constructionist ecofeminists[7] through a validation of non-human nature as an independent entity with a core essence[8] but she also creates a space for Chicana feminists (and, indeed, all others) to have a voice and a story as ecofeminists ban together to rewrite/reweave the oppressive patriarchal myths of life.[9]

It is at the root of the patriarchal myths where one can read the most obvious instances of Anzaldúa's identifications of nature and her contributions to social constructionist ecofeminism. Seen particularly in *Borderlands/La Frontera*, Anzaldúa continually uses the symbols of the serpent and the eagle to align the mestiza with the earth. Since Anzaldúa's faith is rooted in myth, it makes sense that her discussions of a fluid identity are based within pre-Columbian American myths themselves. She notes, in particular, Coatl's descendant Coatlicue as important. Note that this symbol represented by Mother Earth seems the first link in establishing the connection with the natural world currently lacking in social constructionist ecofeminism. This particular symbol, as Anzaldúa attempts to write it back into our mythos, represents not only the idea of a fluid self so pronounced in social constructionist ecofeminism (Coatlicue was both male and female) but also the earth as an agent with a fluid identity as well. In fact, Anzaldúa says that "Coatlicue is the mountain, the Earth Mother who conceived all celestial beings out of her cavernous womb. Goddess of birth and death, Coatlicue gives and takes away life; she is the incarnation of cosmic processes"[10] and also that "Coatlicue depicts the contradictory. . . she is a symbol of the fusion of opposites: the eagle and the serpent, heaven and the underworld, life and death."[11] Coatlicue breaks down dichotomies by representing a fusion of all identities, with that fusion representing a third, a border, identity[12]. Here in particular is where we might mark Anzaldúa's associations with social constructionist ecofeminists.

However, unlike the tendency of social constructionists to deny significance to non-human nature as an entity, Anzaldúa's rewoven myth of Coalticue in itself lends significance to the natural world. The reason Anzaldúa's choice of symbol is so important is because Coatlicue represents something more than merely a symbol. She is not only a reflection of our own social construction but, since social constructionists believe that fluid identity creates higher awareness of the world, Coatlicue, in particular, as the earth, establishes a higher awareness of non-human nature as well. Anzaldúa goes beyond what Joan W. Scott has noted as "an analysis of constructions of power" [13] to establish a space for dialogue with the earth for those coming to terms with their own fluid identities which have been oppressed in some way by cultural myths (be they women, people of color, queer, etc.). Since Anzaldúa places herself, and fellow Chicanas/os, within a third perspective as well—she herself simultaneously finding pieces of herself in brown, white, straight, gay, man's, and woman's cultures[14]—she also creates a space within which those who find themselves on the border can speak to and participate within ecofeminism.

The way this space is created is by encouraging a dialogue with the natural world and understanding that all life, be it human or non-human, is connected; thus, within the realms of social constructionist ecofeminism, adding an additional perspective with the ability to see non-human nature as wholly significant as an entity within itself by way of establishing a relationship with it and feeling the need to hear its voice. One tenet of ecocriticism and ecofeminism alike, particularly in this age of environmental crisis, is fostering a mutual relationship between humans and the world that, according to Cheryll Glotfelty, "takes as its subject the interconnections between nature and culture" and "negotiates between the human and the nonhuman."[15] Establishing this relationship is important because, as Christopher Manes notes, in his essay "Nature and Silence," "We can . . . safely agree with Hans Peter Duerr when he says that 'people do not exploit a nature that speaks to them.'"[16] Manes explores the idea that nature once was animated and was allowed a voice. Patriarchy then distorted nature's voice and stripped nature of its animation, leaving only an entity[17] to be conquered and domesticated—a symbol whose new story was man's story—which could now be used as a tool of oppression (particularly in its connection with women, people of color, etc, who, through that connection, could also be silenced). Thus, Manes concludes by asking how we should go about communicating with nature and who should be doing that communicating.[18] For ecofeminism, that voice communicating with nature should be one that has also been oppressed by patriarchy and by those same myths of identity usurpation. In her books, Anzaldúa clearly gives that privilege of communication to the Chicana specifically and to all "others" in general.[19] To them, nature's voice is still speaking.

Anzaldúa writes the relationship between Chicana and the earth similar to that of the *curandera* (medicine woman), in that, *curandera* must know the earth and its herbs so that she can then use those herbs to heal. In much the same way, Chicanas must understand Coatlicue and use that knowledge to heal the rift placed between humans and nature's voice through patriarchy's dominating use of one historical story/mythos. Likewise, in interviews with AnaLouise Keating between 1998 and 1999, Anzaldúa notes feeling a "deep connection" with nature but:

> This society doesn't encourage that kind of thing. Because we live in an accelerated age, we have so much thrown at us that there's no time to just look at the sky . . . The connections are there, the signs I read in the environment—if a snake crosses my path when I'm walking across Lighthouse Field, it means something to me. I'll look at that tree silhouetted by the sun, and its design says something to me, to my soul, which I then have to decipher. We get these messages from nature, from the creative consciousness or whatever you want to call the intelligence of the universe. It's constantly speaking to us but we don't listen, we don't look.[20]

Since Anzaldúa elsewhere identifies the "we" in her writing as representing the Chicana community,[21] the reader must also assume the same here and that nature is speaking directly to a Chicana ear who both, because of mutual oppression, is allowed to hear but who also, because of participation within that oppressive culture, must learn again to listen. It is the characteristic of being the "voice at the edge of things,"[22] trying to say something while no one is listening that both the Chicana and the Earth share.[23] But, at the same time she calls for Chicanas to listen, she locates that missing core essence in nature that *can* speak, that isn't created by humans, that is active and is calling for action.

Thus, there is hope of regaining clear audience of that voice and of creating within social constructionist ecofeminism a realm which sees nature as an independent entity and not merely a construct. To illustrate, Anzaldúa remembers a red snake once crossing her path and "[t]he direction of its movement, its pace, its colors, the 'mood' of the trees and the wind and the snake—they all 'spoke' to me, told me things. I look for omens everywhere, everywhere catch a glimpse of the patterns and cycles of my life . . . I remember listening to the voices of the wind as a child and understanding its messages."[24] She could understand its message because it is a message that she already partially knew, the message of silencing from other sectors and of an attempt to negotiate identity, to regain power and to heal the wounds. Scholars of Anzaldúa's work must also note here that, in *This Bridge Called My Back* (1987), she calls for her readers to listen to the queer voice and to the voices of those who are part of all cultures because there will be no healing until we can stop putting parts of the whole self down.[25] Just as social ecofeminist Dorothy Dinnerstein shows that it is "counterproductive for half of reality to try to dominate the other half,"[26] Anzaldúa opens up that statement to encompass the whole self—including the earth—and not just parts, for the healing process. Those "parts" might either be queer, mestiza, or of Nature, but that interchangeability is the hope in Anzaldúa and in ecofeminism.

One of the problems that ecofeminists attempt to counter is that our patriarchal cultures try to *deny* the interchangeability of those parts, as stated earlier, by silencing all of them. Recognizing this, Anzaldúa, immediately after remembering hearing nature's voice as a child, turns her attention to that very same ecofeminist critique:

> We're not supposed to remember such otherworldy events. We're supposed to ignore, forget, kill those fleeting images of the soul's presence and of the spirit's presence. We've been taught that the spirit is outside our bodies or above our heads somewhere up in the sky with God. We're supposed to forget that every cell in our bodies, every bone and bird and worm has a spirit.[27]

Significant in this statement is not only the cultural critique which sets both Chicanas and the earth against oppressive constructions of their identities but also the recognition of a spirituality and a connectedness with the life of everything on earth (a form of re-animation which Manes had found lacking). Apparent in the above quote is an animation which comes from the ascription of spirituality and, thus, the location of the earth and everything in it as moral agents[28]. Likewise, ecofeminism "rests on the claims that women and other Others are full moral agents" and that all living things deserve "moral consideration".[29]

The root of Anzaldúa's connection with the earth comes from the ascription of just such a morality—a self-identified reliance on the earth religions of her Indian ancestry.[30] Hence, in various interviews from as early as 1983, when asked about spirituality in her life, Anzaldúa locates it in the natural environment surrounding her. In an interview with Kim Irving, Anzaldúa explains that "Everything has a meaning. Everything is interconnected to me, spirituality and being spiritual means to be aware of the interconnections between things."[31] In this moment, recognizing multiplicity means recognizing the interplay of spirit (nature being one among many, but an entity nonetheless). In fact, not only does she establish the spirituality of everything, but in an interview with Christine Weiland in 1983, Anzaldúa also rewrites the biblical story of life's inception to encompass that multiplicity and interconnectedness. Here she erases God's figure and voice ("In the beginning was the word and the word was with God and the word was God"[32]) to replace it with nature's:

> [I]n the beginning was the sound, the vibration—a rock, a plant, an animal, a human, a particular area. That vibration is like the song of its being, its heartbeat, its rhythm. A lot of the ideas that have come up in the autobiography are spiritual ideas. Especially, the idea that everything is spiritual, that I'm a speck of this soul—which is what Native Americans have always recognized, they've always respected the elements—nothing is alien, nothing is strange. . . . Everything is my relative; I'm related to everything.[33]

By associating the morality in nature with the lessons of Indian earth religions and heritage, Anzaldúa again creates a space where Chicanas, like herself, and all "others" can actively participate in ecofeminist pursuits and oppose oppressive patriarchal mythmaking.

The validity of that participation comes from the joint construction of identity politics for both the "other" and nature. Thus, not only does Anzaldúa align herself with the tenets of ecofeminism in terms of recognizing nature's voice and soul, but also in terms of the mutual definition and oppression of women, nature, and indeed *any* Other, as they are marked as lesser and more primitive. Again Anzaldúa takes the patriarchal myths and rewrites them so that the voices of the "other" and of the natural world can be empowered. This shared battle for a voice and alignment of Chicanas with Coatlicue within that battle happens in a few distinct stages: identity construction, malleability/fluidity as a process of that construction and, finally, the feeling that one is connected with nature as a fellow being. A similar set of stages can be found in Rachel Carson's ecocritical book *Silent Spring* (1962) where Carson calls for a rewriting of man's relationship to the world through an evaluation of the harmful use of pesticides. In *Silent Spring*, Carson explores, just as we have noted Anzaldúa does, the ways in which, since there is a spirituality in everything, we are connected to each part of nature in a mutually respectful relationship. When we allow ourselves to connect with our surroundings, the physical environments within which we place ourselves or find ourselves placed, shape our identities in concrete ways. And, because that environment is continually changing (whether by our own movement to different places, a change in seasons, or a change in our environment caused by the effects of global warming, for instance), so are our identities. Since the two (our identity and nature) are so intertwined, ecofeminists, as well as ecocritics, feel as though their identities are part *of* nature or at least in part *with* nature (again, the interplay being important). With humans and nature affecting one another, we recognize both as historical and interdependent—because independent—beings.

Ecological feminist Chris Cuomo, therefore, argues that "it is worth making connections between . . . movements promoting the flourishing of women and non human life, because both sorts of movements (despite the incredible variety in each) raise deep questions about who we are, as humans, as communities, as dependents, and as complex, *embodied* selves."[34] The title of the second chapter of Anzaldúa and Cherrie Moraga's collaborative work *This Bridge Called My Back: Writings by Radical Women of Color*, "Entering the Lives of Others: Theory in the Flesh," puts the reader in mind of a similar process going on in Anzaldúa's work. The "other" here in the chapter title could, as we have seen, quite literally be the land, and the "theory in the flesh," at least according to Moraga, refers in part to the embodiment of "the land or concrete we grew up on."[35] We can also link this concept with Anzaldúa because, elsewhere in her work, we read this embodiment—and embeddedness—within her own experiences.[36] Fitting with the trend Mary Brady highlights in her study *Extinct Lands, Temporal*

Geographies: Chicana Literature and the Urgency of Space (2002), where she argues that "making identities is integral to making place" and each influences the formation of the other[37] (not where humans construct nature without reciprocity, as other social constructionist ecofeminists have marked it), Anzaldúa notes in an interview with Linda Smuckler in 1982 that she "was born and raised in Jesús María and in Los Vergeles, which means 'the gardens'" and, as a result of where she was raised, "felt very much connected with the sky and the trees and the dirt."[38] In *Borderlands/La Frontera*, while looking for a ground on which to stand[39] (whether referring to a political station or literal earth), when Anzaldúa left "the garden," she "did not leave all the parts of [herself]; [She] kept the ground of [her] own being. On it [she] walked away, taking with [her] the land, the Valley, Texas."[40] As to the construction of her identity, in 1987, Anzaldúa notes the following: "[S]uddenly I feel everything rushing to a center, a nucleus. All the lost pieces of myself coming flying from the deserts and the mountains and the valleys, magnetized toward that center. Completa."[41] Her identity along with the landscape of various places all combine to make her complete. Both are integral to the formation of the other.

The second and third parts of this cycle of identity politics refers to the idea that, as our environments change, so do our identities as humans and, as a result, humans feel as though they are part of nature. Regarding identity, Anzaldúa argues that it "is sort of like a river. It's one and it's flowing, and it's a process."[42] Further, just as identity is a process, Anzaldúa sees (as Mary Pat Brady has seen in other Chicana literature) places as "processes too,"[45] whether the land itself is changed by the human process of farming and its cycles of growth, death, decay, and birth[44] *or* changed by patriarchal development and destruction as we will explore in a moment. As a consequence, the Tejana Chicana specifically and the Chicana/o in general, at least according to Anzaldúa, feel as though they are part of the land. In *Borderlands/La Frontera*, Anzaldúa admittedly "learns to transform the small 'I' into the total Self"[45] in that her identity moves from one of just self-realization to a realization that she is also part of the trees, of coyotes, and of other people. Very graphically, Anzaldúa notes not only that her "heart surges to the beat of the sea,"[46] and that "*[l]a madre naturaleza* succored me, allowed me to grow roots that anchored me to the earth,"[47] but also notes how, being bitten by a snake as a small child, she awoke the next morning feeling that she was a snake now as well.[48] Whether the snake here represents the creatures of the earth or Mexican culture, through the bite she learned to assimilate its (the animal's/Nature's) soul. Additionally, as she is reaching out to all "others," this assimilation can happen on all levels.

Despite arguments that ecofeminism continues to mark differences between the essence of women/nature from men/culture, that essentialism is neither the message of ecofeminism nor Anzaldúa here. Ecofeminists, instead, are interested in patriarchal constructions of both women and nature and how oppressive techniques are used to control both through the "dualistic construction and maintenance of inferior, devalued, or pathologized/naturalized Others."[49] Understanding that there are links in the domination of both women and nature, ecofeminists attempt to reclaim an association with the natural world in order to debunk those patriarchal myths of power. In other words, according to Carolyn Sachs, in *Gendered Fields: Rural Women, Agriculture, and Environment* (1996), ecofeminists "propose that through embracing, celebrating, and redefining women's relations with nature these connections can offer potential emancipation for both women and nature."[50] At the same time, it's the oppression of both women and the land that allow cultural critics/feminists/queer/border people to criticize both cultures. Moments like this allow ecofeminists to alter dominating dualities of nature/culture to create a third state, on the border[51].

In fact, ecofeminists, as I see Anzaldúa, note a need for the alteration of such dominating dualities because, until effectively changed, they lead to the mutual oppression and destruction of both nature, other Others, and, in fact, men as well as they are also limited to a particular identity as oppressors. In *Borderlands*, Anzaldúa marks patriarchy's common wounding, violation and fear of all others (both human and non-human).[52] In what seems an attempt to "make the world a little cleaner and a little safer and stop the destruction,"[53] Anzaldúa identifies the wounds to both herself and to nature in several specific instances. In one such instance, she recalls a memory from childhood: "I was in Prospect Park in Brooklyn for a picnic [sic] everyone was smoking cigarettes and putting them out in the grass. My whole body reacted: I could feel the pain of the grass. These people were turning their live cigarettes on it."[54] Though the pain she felt is partially due to the connection between identities explained earlier, ecofeminists also view moments like the one Anzaldúa mentions as indicative of a larger destruction where nature is no longer valued and, thus, should be destroyed in the name of industrialization and expansion. Vandana Shiva, a scholar of third world ecofeminism, locates "the dominant mode of development as Western, patriarchal and based on a reductionist model of science and technology that serves the global market and is effectively destructive for women, nature, and all 'others.'"[55] Along this vein, Anzaldúa begins *Borderlands* by reminding her readers of the colonization and conquest of Mexican territory and Mexican people in 1848.[56] The focus on numerous forms of oppression in ecofeminism, as noted by Chris Cuomo, has been the focus of radical women of color since around 1985.[57] Though she has yet to be intricately tied into the ecofeminist movement, I would argue that Anzaldúa is doing the work of ecofeminism in the years prior to and around the time Cuomo identifies, as evidenced through interviews and her work *Borderlands*.

Since the future of Chicanos, other Others, and our natural environment hang in the balance, acknowledging that only further destruction will follow until the current myths of power are debunked is of utmost importance for ecofeminism. First noting the destruction, Anzaldúa comments that "White America has only attended to the body of the earth in order to exploit it, never to succor it or to be nurtured in it."[58] Building upon this idea, she goes on to state a hope in the spiritual leadership of multicultural peoples: "Let us hope that the left hand, that of darkness, or femaleness, of 'primitiveness,' can divert the indifferent, right handed, 'rational' suicidal drive that, unchecked, could blow us into acid rain in a fraction of a millisecond."[59] For Anzaldúa, it is the duty of the "Other" to create change and to overpower the right hand of patriarchy if we are to ever live in an ecological and state.[60] We might read, then, the following statement not only as a call to Chicana feminists but as a legitimizing statement for the inclusion of those Chicana feminists and other Others within the ecofeminist movement: "*Together* we form a vision which spans from the self-love of our colored skins, to the respect of our foremothers who kept the embers of revolution burning, to our reverence for the trees—the final reminder of our rightful place on this planet."[61] Hence, even when nominally identifying with the ecofeminist movement (as evidenced in the quote to begin this paper), Anzaldúa records a responsibility for changing the world under the new sixth sun and for women to continue taking care of the earth. After all, as Chris Cuomo astutely asks: "If an ethic does not aim to prioritize the flourishing of moral agents and the entities that they value deeply for noninstrumental reasons; and entities upon which they rely for life itself; and entities that are irreplaceable, can feel pain, and are friend and kin to humans—what good is it?"[62]

Based on ecofeminism and on Anzaldúa's arguments, such a movement without empathy for other Others would be ineffective. Rhetorical questions aside, the issue becomes how we Others can actively seek to acknowledge that responsibility by effecting change. The question becomes, *how* are we to overpower the patriarchal hand? For some it has been disavowal of a relationship with nature and for others the answer has been to rewrite the patriarchal story. According to Ursula K. LeGuin, in her article "The Carrier Bag of Fiction" (1996), many of us have become trapped by the idea that a story must have conflict and that a story must have a hero.[63] Thus, our stories (and "our" implies that at least those of us who live in first world countries are complicit in the furthering of these stories) have become ones of "bashing, sticking, thrusting, killing."[64] They have become "killer stories."[65] For LeGuin it's the story that makes all the difference. So, in order to change our future trajectory and to overpower the right hand of patriarchy before it is too late, we must rewrite those stories and change them into life stories, stories that, for LeGuin, carry energy and give voice back to those from whom it was usurped. The solution for ecofeminists is to "seek the nature, subject, words of the other story, the untold one, the life story."[66] Mythmaking and story weaving must come back into the hands of the silenced and the oppressed. As you may recall, Anzaldúa is *ready* to create that new story.

When speaking with Debbie Blake and Carmen Abrego in an interview in 1994, Anzaldúa states: "Myths and fictions create reality, and these myths and fictions are used against women and against certain races to control, regulate, and manipulate us. I'm rewriting the myths, using the myths back against the oppressors."[67] She acknowledges that figures in these myths (which could potentially be empowering for women and for nature) are being written from a patriarchal perspective and divided up/silenced.[68] Just as LeGuin did, Anzaldúa sees it as her duty to "put us back together again."[69] In doing so and in resituating the figures in the patriarchal myths Anzaldúa figures out ways in which to "formulate theories about where the oppressions connect and where [she could] create empowering ways—whether physical, emotional, derived from activism or from writing."[70] There is the possibility of writing stories that have the ability to (re)inscribe our identity prior to the domination and oppressions of patriarchy and that can solidify a relationship with Coatlicue.

Living on the border, for Anzaldúa and for Chicana/o culture, means living in a space that has one foot on brown soil (with all of its associations and connotations) and one foot on white (with all of its associations/connotations as well)—a space that incorporates, according to Benay Blend, "ancient and modern cultural beliefs"[71]. As such, the land on the border actually provides the site of inquisition for the patriarchal myths on both sides of the border and physically provides a space in which fluidity/fusion/liminality is empowering—even strong enough to speak for the (now) unspoken. In fact, this space allows figures like Anzaldúa to "interpret a relationship with the land that continues tradition yet introduces change. A borderland—between countries, between cultures, between past and present, and between genders as well as genres . . . [and] offers, then, a new creative space for multiple points of view."[72] For those who can and will listen to earth's story, as Anzaldúa does and as she calls for fellow border people to do, there are many stories to be told as well as many voices to be heard. Recognizing that those stories need to be written is the first step in challenging the tactics of oppression present in the myths that create our everyday lived experiences.

It is for just such a reason that Anzaldúa declares: "for images, words, stories to have . . . transformative power, they must arise from the human body—flesh and bone—and from the Earth's body—stone, sky, liquid, soil."[73] Mirroring LeGuin's call for ecofeminist activity in writing, Anzaldúa also informs her readers that, if we wish to rid ourselves of the patriarchal domination then "[w]e have to make up new myths and new stories, we have to create more of a balance."[74] As Anzaldúa urges here,[75] for us to change culture and rewrite culture, ecofeminists must encourage the Other to begin using the cultural tools of patriarchal oppression (i.e. the link with nature) as something empowering rather than as something to deny for fear of that link—as a myth that can be rewritten and turned around to counter those same patriarchal assumptions. Because of Anzaldúa and what appears to be her adherence to ecofeminist tenets, now mestiza and native women are taking up pens and "reclaiming the agency of reinscribing, taking off their inscriptions and reinscribing ourselves, our identities, our own cultures."[76]

Based on a close reading of Gloria Anzaldúa's *Borderlands/La Frontera* and *Interviews/Entrevistas*, her detailed descriptions of the *mestiza*/border experiences and her call to action in not only locating one's experiences deep within the earth itself but also in a responsibility to heal the earth definitely mark her as someone sympathetic to the ecofeminist cause. She calls for her readers to join her as they "root [them]selves in the mythological soil and soul of this continent,"[77] just as she had allowed roots to anchor her own body to the earth.[78] Despite such seemingly obvious connections, Anzaldúa scholars, like Cassie Premo Steele in *We Heal From Memory: Sexton, Lorde, Anzaldúa, and the Poetry of Witness* (2000), argue that the reconstruction of history is merely a process for Anzaldúa as she looks to the future. Steele argues that the reconnection with the earth (and, thus, the reconstruction of myths) is merely a means to an end to be left behind eventually[79] and did not read that reconnection, as I argue in this essay that it should be read, as something intricately linked to future survival. Throughout this chapter we have seen the ways in which Anzaldúa seems to align herself with the tenets of ecofeminism in general: hearing nature and allowing it to speak and recognizing the interconnectedness of life. We have seen, as well, her specific connections to the social constructionist ecofeminist movement in her destabilization of dichotomies and interest in the fluidity of identity. Most importantly, however, we have seen the ways in which Anzaldúa's (and, as she locates it, all border people's) relationship with Coatlicue, mythmaking, and the earth create a new space from within that social ecofeminism to view nature as independent and our connections with non-human nature to be empowering. That connection and the allowance of space for the pens of other Chicana feminists to rewrite culture, is Anzaldúa's radically active gift to ecofeminism: "I write to record what others erase when I speak, to rewrite the stories others have miswritten about me, about you" [80] . . . and we might also add "about the earth."

Notes

1. Gloria Anzaldúa. *Borderlands/La Frontera: The New Mestiza* (San Fransisco: Aunt Lute Books), 1987, 38.
2. Anzaldúa. 49.
3. Anzaldúa. 102-3.
4. Anzaldúa. 38.
5. AnaLouise Keating, ed. *Interviews/ Entrevistas* (New York: Routledge, 2000), 193.
6. Most scholars, like Andrea Parra, have merely noted the "appeal" of ecofeminism to Latin American feminists like Anzaldúa. For more information, see her essay in "Forum on Literatures of the Environment." *PMLA* 114 (Oct. 1999): 1099-1100.
7. Briefly, social constructionist ecofeminists desire to dissolve and deny power to dichotomies, particularly man/woman and culture/nature. They see identity as something which can and does encompass all aspects of life. As those aspects are, themselves, constantly changing, identity is fluid. One critique of social constructionist ecofeminism, however, has been its valorization of human life above non-human life.

8. Arguments have been leveled at social constructionist ecofeminism that, while it sees human identity as fluid with a core central essence, it sees non-human nature as greatly inferior to human nature and significance. This is the point Anzaldúa makes room for in her argument. She effectively creates a space where social constructionist ecofeminists can still see human identity with that same fluidity and also see nature as significant.

9. Jasmin Sydee and Sharon Beder note, in the article "Ecofeminism and Globalism," that women "treated as 'Other", Indigenous women, African-American women and women from the South, it is argued, are still excluded, by material economic forces, from an 're-weaving' that is occurring"—in *Democracy and Nature.* July (2001): 281-302. Room for Othered women to speak about themselves and to connect with nature is yet another realm of Social ecofeminism that Anzaldúa is trying to open up to discussion.

10. Anzaldúa. *Borderlands/La Frontera,* 68.

11. Anzaldúa. 69.

12. Anzaldúa. 46. Here Anzaldúa notes that Coatlicue "simultaneously, depending on the person . . . represents: duality in life, a synthesis of duality, and a third perspective—something more than mere duality or a synthesis of duality."

13. Joan W. Scott. "Multiculturalism and the Politics of Identity." *The Identity in Question.* 61 (1992): 16.

14. Cherrie Moraga and Gloria Anzaldúa, eds. *This Bridge Called My Back: Writings by Radical Women of Color (*Waterton, MA: Persephone Press, 1981), 205.

15. Cheryll Glotfelty, "Introduction: Literary Studies in an Age of Environmental Crisis." *The Ecocriticism Reader.* Cheryll Glotfelty and Harold Fromm, eds. (Athens, GA: University of Georgia Press, 1996), xix.

16. Christopher Manes, "Nature and Silence." *The Ecocriticism Reader.*Cheryll Glotfelty and Harold Fromm, eds. (Athens, GA: University of Georgia Press, 1996), 16.

17. Manes, "Nature and Silence," 26.

18. Manes, 25.

19. Note that, when I refer to Chicana within the paper that Anzaldúa doesn't limit the relationship only to Chicanas/os but to all those on the border, locating themselves within some "othered" existence.

20. Anzaldúa, *Interviews/Entrevistas,* 286.

21. Anzaldúa, 222.

22. Anzaldúa, *Borderlands/La Frontera,* 49.

23. Keep in mind here the hard time Anzaldúa and Cherrie Moraga had getting *This Bridge Called My Back* published, as though, with Chicanas as well, no one cared to hear.

24. Anzaldúa, *Borderlands/La Frontera,* 36.

25. Anzaldúa,, 84.

26. Quoted in Rosemarie Tong. *Feminist Thought.* 2nd ed. (Boulder, CO: Westview Press, 1998), 264.

27. Anzaldúa, *Borderlands/La Frontera,* 36. Here again Anzaldúa notes a core essence/identity within nature that is equal to human essence/identity.

28. Again, Anzaldúa is not essentializing a connection here between women and nature but, instead, showing that both nature and "others" *have* an essence or an independent identity whose voice has been silenced.

29. Chris J. Cuomo, *Feminism and Ecological Communities* (New York: Routledge, 1998), 63.

30. Anzaldúa, *Interviews/ Entrevistas,* 96.

31. Anzaldúa, 9

32. *Holy Bible, The.* King James Version. Rev. C.I. Scofield, ed. (New York: Oxford University Press, 1945), John 1:1.

33. Anzaldúa, *Interviews/Entrevistas*, 100

34. Cuomo, *Femenism and Ecological Communities*, 150

35. Moraga and Anzaldúa, *This Bridge Called My Back* 23

36. Gabriela Arrendondo, Aida Hurtado et al., eds, *Chicana Feminisms* (Durham: Duke University Press, 2003), 116. Here Arrendondo mentions several other Chicana author who located the importance of space and place on identity formation. Some of the ones mentioned are Sandra Cisneros' *House on Mango Street* (1984), Norma Cantú's *Canicula* (1995), Mary Helen Ponce's *Hoyt Street* (1933), and Pat Mora's *House of Houses* (1997).

37. Mary Pat Brady, *Extinct Lands, Temporal Geographies: Chicana Literature and the Urgency of Space* (Durham: Duke University Press, 2002), 52-53. In keeping with this idea, in an interview with AnaLouise Keating in 1991, Anzaldúa noted that the "self extends to the tree. The self does not stop with just you, with your body. The self penetrates other things and they penetrate you" (*Interviews/ Entrevistas* 162).

38. Anzaldúa, *Interviews/Entrevistas* 89

39. Anzaldúa, *Borderlands/La Frontera* 23

40. Anzaldúa, 16

41. Arrendondo, *Chicana Feminisms*, 364

42. Arrendondo, 132

43. Brady, *Extinct Lands*, 112

44. Anzaldúa, *Borderlands/ La Frontera* 91

45. Anzaldúa, 83

46. Anzaldúa, 2

47. Anzaldúa, 1

48. Anzaldúa, 26

49. Cuomo, *Feminism and Ecological Communities*, 24

50. Carolyn Sachs, *Gendered Fields: Rural Women, Agriculture, and Environment* (Boulder, CO: Westview Press, 1996), 30

51. This is the same border in which social constructionist ecofeminists locate identity—a space where life can be female and male, Anglo and Chicano, etc.

52. Anzaldúa, *Borderlands/ La Frontera* 84

53. Anzaldúa, *Interviews/ Entrevistas* 160. Anzaldúa stated this as a goal in an interview with AnaLouise Keating in 1991.

54. Anzaldúa, *Borderlands/ La Frontera* 26

55. Rosi Braidotti, Ewa Charkiewicz et al., eds., *Women, the Environment, and SustainableDevelopment: Towards a Theoretical Synthesis* (Atlantic Highlands, NJ: Zed Books, 1994), 94

56. Cherrie Moraga also noted that the bodies of the earth and of "others" are under patriarchal control when, as highlighted in Brady's book *Extinct Lands, Temporal Geographies*, she is quoted as saying: "Land remains the common ground for all radical action. But land is more than the rocks and trees, the animal and plant life that make up the territory of Aztlán of Navajo Nation or Maya Meso-america. For immigrants and natives alike, land is also the factories where we work, the water our children drink, and the housing project where we live. For women, lesbians, and gay men, land is that physical mass called our bodies. Throughout las Américas, all these 'lands' remain under occupation by a Anglo-centric, patriarchal, imperialist U.S." (166).

57. Cuomo, *Feminism and Ecological Communities*, 33

58. Anzaldúa, *Borderlands/ La Frontera* 68

59. Anzaldúa, 68–9.

60. Again, Anzaldúa is not blaming men for our relationships with one another and with the earth but is locating that blame within patriarchal myths themselves.

61. Anzaldúa, *This Bridge Called My Back,* 196.

62. Cuomo, *Feminism and Ecological Communities,* 65.

63. Ursula K. LeGuin, "The Carrier Bag Theory of Fiction," *The Ecocriticism Reader,* Cheryll Glotfelty and Harold Fromm, eds. (Athens, GA: University of Georgia Press, 1996), 150.

64. LeGuin, 151.

65. LeGuin, 151.

66. LeGuin, 152.

67. Anzaldúa, *Interviews/Entrevistas,* 219.

68. Anzaldúa, 219.

69. Anzaldúa, 220.

70. Anzaldúa, 221.

71, Benay Blend, Barry, "Intersections of Nature and the Self in Chicana Writing," *New Essays in Ecofeminist Literary Critcism.* Glynis Carr, ed. (Lewisburg: Bucknell University Press, 2000), 58.

72. Blend, 56-7.

73. Anzaldúa, *Borderlands/La Frontera,* 75.

74. Anzaldúa, *Interviews/Entrevistas,* 194.

75. Anzaldúa, 221.

76. Anzaldúa, 189.

77. Arrendondo, *Chicana Feminisms*, 366

78. Anzaldúa, *Borderlands/ La Frontera,* 1.

79. Cassie Premo Steele. We Heal From Memory: Sexton, Lorde, Anzaldúa, and the Poetry Of Witness (New York: Palgrave, 2000), 54.

80. Anzaldúa, *This Bridge Called My Back,* 169.

10

Teaching the Trees: How to Be a Female Nature Writer

Joan E. Maloof

1. Get up, go out
2. Love nature
3. Sit down, write words
4. Find your own fresh voice
5. Read a lot, but don't read everything
6. Tell a story and put yourself in it
7. Don't fear the science
8. Be humbled by complexity
9. Try to save the world

1. Get up, go out

Men are expected to be brave and to explore. Women should stay safely protected in the company of others, indoors if at all possible. Although this stereotype is gradually weakening, I think it still exists to some degree in most cultures. Which of these behavior patterns do you think will produce the best nature writers? For a woman to write about nature, then, she must appropriate some so-called male behaviors. Not only must she be brave enough to explore on her own, but more difficult still, she must be brave enough to dismiss the expectations of her culture.

Both John Muir and Henry David Thoreau grew up wandering alone in the woods, and they continued to roam alone and to write about their roamings. This solo roaming takes bravery, even for the statistically larger sex of our species. Honestly, anything could happen out there, to anyone, and having a companion would in many cases increase the chances of survival. But, as any writer, musician or painter can tell you, being alone nurtures creativity. So the brave men frequently set out alone and the result is that some of the best known early American nature writing was done by men.

To be a female nature writer you must shake off the forces that would keep you safe in the company of others. You must be brave, you must explore. William Stafford wrote a poem about a young girl just discovering this way of being, and its rewards. What makes Stafford's poem exciting is that it is about a *girl* who goes into the woods alone. This adds tension. If it had been a young boy we would have shrugged; everyone is used to the idea of a young boy exploring the woods. But Millicent explored the woods on her own, without permission, and there she found the heart of the world:

The Day Millicent Found the World

Every morning Millicent ventured farther
into the woods. At first she stayed
And now not only the giant trees were strange
but the ground at her feet had a velvet nearness;
intricate lines on bark wove messages all
around her. Long strokes of golden sunlight
shifted over her feet and hands. She felt
caught up and breathing in a great powerful embrace.
A birdcall wandered forth at leisurely intervals
from an opening on her right: "Come away, Come away."
Never before had she let herself realize
that she was part of the world and that it would follow
wherever she went. She was part of its breath.

Aunt Dolbee called her back that time, a high
voice tapering faintly among the farthest trees,
"Milli-cent! Milli-cent!" And that time she returned,
but slowly, her dress fluttering along pressing
back branches, her feet stirring up the dark smell
of moss, and her face floating forward, a stranger's
face now, with a new depth in it, into the light.[1]

I am Millicent. I mean, I have gone into the woods alone too. If you are a woman and you try this you will probably experience raised eyebrows and concern (whether feigned or real). "Aren't you afraid?" they will ask. "What if something happens?" You can tell that they'd prefer, like Aunt Dolbee, that you just stay home and do needlepoint. You will find that this reaction is almost universal: young or old, male or female; almost no one will like the idea of you going off alone. My daughter is just as dubious as my husband, or my parents, or my friends.

You must be brave, or some would say callous, enough that the concerns of others are of no concern to you. Ask yourself if they are really afraid for your physical safety, or if deep in their unconscious they aren't perhaps more afraid that you will lose yourself and return with a stranger's face reflecting a new depth. It is threatening when those close to us change and grow. Don't let someone else's fear stop you. Don't be nice enough to stay home. If you do you will have nothing to write about.

Getting up and going out is also about having ideas and following through. Paul Krafel writes about watching vultures circle around a particular cliff at dawn. For weeks he had been watching the spectacle from a distance, but then:

> I hiked to the top of that cliff one morning so I could look straight down onto the backs of a hundred vultures rising toward me. I felt the sunrise's invisible magic on the air; a warm updraft blew against my face. As the vultures rose by me a few feet away, I heard them. They made no call. I heard simply the sound of six feet of wing cutting through the air—a gentle but constant breezy swoosh. And now I know that even on the stillest desert afternoon, the soaring vulture hears not the silence but the constant gentle sound of its wings.[2]

He doesn't mention that he had to set the alarm for five a.m. to get to the top of the cliff in time for sunrise. He doesn't mention the tasks left undone at home, or done by others, so he could make his trek. All we know is that he had an idea and he got up and followed through. Now he has a story.

Some people will be suspicious. They will assume that if you are going off alone it is to meet secretly with someone else. They will suspect that sex must somehow be involved. And, honestly, there is something archetypically sexy about a woman going into the wilds alone. Perhaps it shows that she is the type of woman who breaks rules; or could it be her very vulnerability that is somehow thrilling? Even in Stafford's poem about an innocent young girl there are numerous sexual undertones: the *velvet nearness,* the *long strokes,* the *powerful embrace.* This is nature as lover.

2. Love nature

To be an effective nature writer one must love the wild things and feel that they are loving back. This planet is wildly beautiful. You believe that already or you would never consider making it the central character in your writing. Few pleasures in this life can compare with those moments when what comes through your eyes and your nose and your ears and your skin create an ecstatic hum in the brain's neurons. E. O. Wilson calls this pleasure *biophilia,* literally life-love.[3] The hum of life creates joy because we have literally evolved in life's embrace. We are infants in love with our mother's face.

Now write about what *that* feels like. Why do people line up for hours to see panda cubs? Why do travelers spend great sums of money to go whale watching? Why does waterfront real estate command such high sums? We are in love. Honor that. Write about it.

3. Sit down, write words

The most challenging part about nature writing is that it alternates active, adventurous, body-based pursuits with sedentary, meticulous, intellectual habits. People are usually good at one or the other, but hardly anyone is good at both. And even if you can do both necessary duties, there is the question of how much time to devote to each one. I no longer have the exact quote, but Rick Bass wrote something that I repeat as a kind of mantra: you've got to know when to sit down at your desk, and when to get up from it.

You can't be a nature writer if you get up and go out *all* the time, because eventually you will have to sit down and put words on paper. As Anne Lamott advises, "You simply keep putting down one damn word after the other, as you hear them, as they come to you."[4] But the words won't come unless you sit down in silence and wait for them. Writing is all about words and silence is the space where words appear. Just as a painter does not begin a painting without a blank canvas, you will not feel the magic of the words bubbling up from nowhere unless you give them a quiet pool in which to rise. No one taught me this in school; our culture seems to place no value in silence. If you want to write, but you don't know what words to use, just be silent for a time. The words will come.

Unfortunately for you, the world won't want you to sit down in silence waiting for words to come. The pets will want attention, your phone will ring, the bathroom faucet will drip. But if you never sit down with pencil to paper or fingers to keyboard you will never be a writer, no matter how adventurous you are, or what great thoughts you think.

Many people have assumed that the actual sitting down part is much harder for women because of the children or the domestic chores. I do think it's more difficult for women, but not for those reasons. Every person on Earth has several hundred good reasons not to sit down and write. The trick is being able to leave tasks left undone without feeling guilt. I think the average woman is just more susceptible to self-imposed guilt than the average man.

Some people hesitate, they do not sit down to begin writing because they have no idea what they will write. This is normal and it is nothing to be afraid of. Here is what I would say to them: *something is more important to you this very day than it has ever been in your life*. Now ask yourself what that one thing is. It doesn't have to be big or important; it could at first seem very small and insignificant. It could be the sight of the first woolly bear caterpillar of the year, or the splinter you just got in your finger, or the vultures flying in the distance, it doesn't matter. On this day you feel differently about vultures or splinters or woolly bears than you have ever felt before. So that is where you will begin. Of course you probably still don't know what woolly bears have to do with anything, but when you begin writing you will find out. And that's when writing makes your heart sing—when the thing that was there all along, but hidden, shows itself to you. Sometimes you have to stop and stare out into space, pretend you're not watching, to coax it out a bit. Finally you get a glimpse of truth, or that moment's truth anyway, and the words rush and tumble so quickly that you must get them quickly on paper before they disappear. Joy! You have captured a likeness of the secretive beast. The Chinese poet Lu Chi says, "Each artist has his own way to magic."[5] This is mine.

4. Find your own fresh voice

There is a section in Henry David Thoreau's essay, *The Succession of Forest Trees* that I simply adore:

> See how artfully the seed of a cherry is placed in order that a bird may be compelled to transport it,—in the very midst of a tempting pericarp, so that the creature that must devour this must commonly take the stone also into its mouth or bill. If you ever ate a cherry, and did not make two bites of it, you must have perceived it,—right in the centre of the luscious morsel, a large earthy residuum left on the tongue.[6]

It continues so brilliantly that I can barely bring myself to stop, but this much at least gets the point across. And the point is that as perfectly beautiful as this is, it sounds nothing at all like contemporary nature writing. If you model your nature writing on Thoreau—the most well known nature writer in America—you will be obsolete before you begin. Literature has changed. You must still get up and go out, you must still love nature, you must still sit down and write, but the way you write must be your own fresh voice.

I once attended a seminar where a publishing agent was supposed to be sharing the real, inside story about the publishing business. She flatly stated that she didn't think nature writing would ever sell big. "But what about Rachel Carson?" the audience of female nature writers almost blurted in unison.

"Yes," said the agent, "but you know, I was looking at one of her books the other day, and if she were writing now I'm not sure she would be picked up by a publisher."

Shocked and dismayed is the sort of expression a good writer is not supposed to use, but it expresses the sentiment of that audience exactly. Of course I didn't want to believe the agent either, but I tried to be open minded enough to consider what she had said. I have a copy of *Silent Spring* and, admittedly, I have never read it from cover to cover. I tried again, but I didn't make it through this time either. If I were the acquisitions editor at a press would I push it forward? Perhaps not. Not now. Her writing was as important as it was because of when it was. But literature changes, and if you write like Carson today you probably won't be able to quit your day job and buy a house in Maine as she did. But that doesn't mean you have to stop writing. Like the moths and the finches, writing evolves.

5. Tell a story and put yourself in it

After my book about trees was published,[7] people would ask me about *other* tree books. "Have you read *Tree: a Life Story*?"[8] someone asked. No, I hadn't. But soon I had my library copy in hand. Faculty are allowed to keep books from the university library for almost a year. Some books get inhaled the moment I get them home and returned a few days later, but *Tree* kept gathering dust under my bed. Some evenings I would wipe it off and start reading again, but before long I would drift off to sleep, and the next day I didn't feel compelled to reach for it again. There's no doubt the book was well researched—it had many more facts than my volume—but there was no person telling the story. There was not even a tree telling the story. There was just this disembodied narrator who never seemed to get emotional about anything. I didn't want to be seated next to that narrator at a dinner party. I just knew that if I was seated next to him I would embarrass myself by yawning into my port. So smart, but . . . I want to sit next to Annie Dillard instead. When she tells a story she is right there in it:

> Someday, I had been telling myself for weeks, someday a muskrat is going to swim right through that channel in the cattails, and I am going to see it. That is precisely what happened. I looked up into the channel for a muskrat, and there it came, swimming right toward me. . . . I could just look and look. . . . I felt such a rush of pure energy I thought I would not need to breathe for days.[9]

Now I've seen plenty of muskrats, and I've never reacted in quite that way, but suddenly I want to go hiking with this woman. I don't want to leave her side. I'm wide awake and I don't think it's the chocolate truffle I just ate.

Women are so used to being in their complicated bodies that it naturally spills over into more embodied writing. This is one sphere in which we have an advantage. Before you object to my sexism, however, I want to point out that there are boring writers of both sexes, and some male writers are so present in their writing that I am in love with them even before I get the dinner invitation. Richard Nelson, for example:

> The doe is now ten feet from me. She never pauses or looks away. Her feet punch down mechanically into the snow, coming closer and closer, until they are less than a yard from my own. Then she stops, stretches her neck calmly toward me, and lifts her nose.
>
> There is not the slightest question in my mind, as if this was sure to happen and I have known all along exactly what to do. I slowly raise my hand and reach out.
>
> And my fingers touch the soft, dry, gently needling fur on top of the deer's head, and press down the living warmth of the flesh underneath.
>
> She makes no move and shows no fear, but I can feel the flaming strength and tension that flow in her wild body like no other animal I have touched. Time expands and I am suspended in the clear reality of the moment.[10]

I am swooning. There is no doubt that he is in this perfect story.

6. Don't fear the science

Unless you are writing a field guide or a text book, you will need to have a story. Of course you already have one that no one else has—*your* story. But if you've already fully told that story (which is, of course, impossible) then you'll have to tell another story. And this is the biggest reason you should embrace science: it uncovers wonderful stories.

By now you have heard of the lovely symbiosis between flowers and bees—the bees come to flowers for nectar and unwittingly assist the flowers in sexual reproduction. But unless you've been reading the science journals you probably don't know about the symbiosis between a certain wasp and a certain virus. (Hint: your readers probably haven't been reading science journals either so this story will be new to them too.) Neither wasp nor virus can reproduce without the other, their DNA is literally entwined. The wasp builds the virus inside her ovaries alongside her eggs. Her eggs are destined to be inserted into a soft caterpillar where the little larvae that hatch from the eggs can use the caterpillar's body as a sort of nutritious pâté. When the larvae mature they hatch from the caterpillar's body and fly away carrying the DNA for the next generation of virus particles. But what does the virus do for the wasp? Without the virus the caterpillar's immune system would react to the foreign wasp eggs and kill them. But when the virus enters the caterpillar with the eggs the caterpillar's immune system will focus on the virus and ignore the eggs. The virus is destroyed and literally gives up its life for the sake of the little wasp eggs. But inside the eggs, deep inside the ovaries of the developing female wasps, is the genetic code for the next generation of viral particles. If the wasps live to fly, so will the virus.[11]

See? Science isn't boring at all. There are all these wonderful scientists working very hard in their laboratories just to uncover stories for you. And in the strange way that culture and writing works together, the very people who uncover these wonderful stories are encouraged to print them places where the typical nature lover will never get to read them. Not only that, but they are encouraged to write the stories in the driest way possible. They are not *allowed* to place themselves in the story. It took them years to figure out what was happening, but you're the one that gets to write: "Holy God in heaven, how did something so amazingly complex ever come to be? And what more is there that we have no idea of yet?"

Historically, women have not been as active in the sciences as men, but that is changing quickly. In the University where I teach, proportionally more women than men go on to graduate school in the sciences.

7. Be humbled by complexity

Humans tend to get a little puffed out about how smart they are. We have invented amazing things. We have come to understand the physical world in ways that were inconceivable just a few hundred years ago. But the comings and goings of living things, on just a single acre of land, are still too complex for our most sophisticated computer programs to model. There are just too many variables, and despite the diligent work of many scientists, we still lack an understanding of many basic natural events. There are more unknowns in any natural environment than there are knowns. For instance, on the piece of Earth where I have been living for twenty years the dragonflies appear every June. The population of dragonflies gets steadily larger until September, when the population begins to shrink. But this year, *this year*, one year out of twenty, there were more dragonflies than anyone had ever seen. Every cornstalk had a dragonfly perched atop it. Why, just this year, were there so many dragonflies? Here is the truth: no one knows. And what effects will that population explosion of dragonflies have on next year's flora and fauna? Another truth: no one knows. We can deny these truths by insisting that someone, somewhere, must know. Or we can practice that trait so rare in humans: humility.

It is when humans ignore humility, and pretend that they understand everything, that unexpected complications arise to teach the hard lesson of humility once again. Take, for example, what happened in 1955. Humans had invented a chemical called DDT that could kill mosquitoes. In Borneo mosquitoes spread deadly malaria, so the World Health Organization sprayed DDT over the tropical island. The incidence of malaria was reduced, but soon the villager's thatched roofs caved in. It turns out that a caterpillar that feeds on the thatch was normally kept in check by a parasitic wasp, but the DDT killed the wasps along with the mosquitoes. No one predicted this. Nor did they predict that the insecticide coated insects would be eaten by lizards that would in turn be eaten by cats. And, likewise, no one predicted that the death of the cats, from DDT, would lead to a population explosion of plague carrying rats. Understandably, the World Health Organization didn't want to publish much about this debacle. But you can. Humility comes more easily to the powerless, and females have historically had less power, at least financially and politically, than males. So perhaps we have an advantage here. It was a humble child, after all, who was not afraid to say that the emperor wore no clothes. Be the voice that tells us what we don't know; help humble us.

8. Read a lot, but don't try to read everything

I probably don't have to advise you to read a lot, because if you have read this far it is likely that you are one of those under the spell of the sensuous shapes we call letters. Reading brings you great pleasure, and that is a good thing. But the words of others are like feathers—with the right number of them you can soar to unexpected heights, but with an excess it is difficult to get off the ground. If you really want to be a writer, at some point you must stop reading and start writing. Many would-be writers have a fear of writing something that has already been written, so they feel compelled to read that next book, just to make sure that it isn't the one they wanted to write. But you know what? It isn't. The book you are reading now is amazing, and it contains many wonderful things, but it doesn't say them exactly like you'd say them. And even if *your* book is out there somewhere, so what. In 2005 four different books were published about the art and science of birdsong. All of them seem to be selling well. Those authors did not let the fear of redundancy stop them. We can use more than one book about everything. Realize that you can't read everything and only then start writing, for there is no end to the words streaming out of our culture. If you want to write you must jump into the water, be a part of the stream.

Men are perhaps at an advantage here with their bravery and "devil-may-care" attitude. (Note that the birdsong books were all by men.) But we can do it too. With a bit of prodding we can leap from the high dive with the rest of them.

9. Try to save the world

Many women find that nurturing comes naturally to them, and this planet is in serious need of nurturing. Nature is not just beautiful and complex, it is our very lifeblood. It is the air we breathe, the water we drink, the thoughts we think. We tend to forget this if we are not reminded—and apparently we are not reminded enough. The result of our ignorance is tainting the blood of our newborns: babies are born with mercury and jet fuel additives in their veins. The coral reefs are dying bit by bit, day by day. The butterflies are sprayed with insecticide, from planes. This is real. And this is why Robert Pyle says, "nature writing must be more than an excuse for spending time pleasantly."[12] It is important work, and it deserves every ounce of your skill. Next to loving each other, I think that trying to save some of this beautiful, complex, joyful, place is the most important work there is. What hope have we if our source of nourishment and creativity runs dry? Making our interconnectedness and our fragility palpable is a noble calling.

Millicent got up, she went out, and she obviously loves nature. She is off to a good start. I think she'll make a fine nature writer.

Notes

1. William Stafford, *The Way It Is: New and Selected Poems* (Saint Paul: Graywolf, 1999), 23–24.

2. Paul Krafel, *Seeing Nature: Deliberate Encounters with the Visible World* (White River Junction, VT: Chelsea Green, 1999), 36.

3. E. O. Wilson, *Biophilia* (Cambridge, MA: Harvard University Press, 1984).

4. Anne Lamott, *Bird by Bird: Some Instructions on Writing and Life* (New York: Anchor Books, 1995), 236.

5. Lu Chi, "Rhymeprose on Literature," Achilles Fang, trans. *The New Directions Anthology of Classical Chinese Poetry* (New York: New Directions, 2003), 183.

6. Henry David Thoreau, "The Succession of Forest Trees," *Natural History Essays* (Salt Lake City: Peregrine Smith Books, reprint edition, 1989), 76.

7. Joan Maloof, *Teaching the Trees: Lessons from the Forest* (Athens: University of Georgia Press, 2005).

8. David Suzuki and Wayne Grady, *Tree: a Life Story* (Vancouver: Greystone Books, 2004).

9. Annie Dillard, *Pilgrim at Tinker Creek* (New York: Harper's Magazine Press, 1974), 192.

10. Richard Nelson, *The Island Within* (New York: Vintage Books, 1989), 274–75.

11. David Shiga, "Parasitoid Wasps use Viruses as a Weapon," *Science News* 167 (2005): 136–37.

12. Robert Michael Pyle, *Walking the High Ridge: Life as a Field Trip* (Minneapolis: Milkweed Editions, 2000), 113.

11

Confessions of an Ecofeminist

Rosemarie Rowley

I was born towards mid-century, in 1942, and although I grew up in the capital city of Dublin, Ireland, my background was rural and my family and I were isolated and apart from the twentieth century depredations which have left such a mark on our planet. My journey, then, like Blake's, was from Innocence to Experience, as, at the age of twenty-one, I left idyllic Ireland, which was still unspoilt, for the industrial city of Birmingham, in Great Britain, a place which had experienced to the full, the industrial revolution, which not only left its mark on the landscape, but on the people who lived there.

Nothing in my background had prepared me for this onslaught of the material world, not only had my parents originated from the country, during wartime we had become accustomed, as a family, to frugality and restraint. The beautiful hills of Dublin and the as yet unpolluted sea were the backdrop to my emotional landscape, which was in tune with Nature to a sensitive degree. Not only that, but my father was a traditional musician, and from childhood our house had been full of Irish music with its rhythms and beautiful cadences. Neither did my background indicate I might become feminist, I had a wonderful role model in an aunt who became a songwriter in America, while my father encouraged all his children, and especially his daughters into education, something which he went out and worked very hard for in those days. So how did I become an ecofeminist?

By nature romantic, I became attached to a young man whose uncle had often visited our house to play flute music—by inference, I thought this nephew also belonged to this musical and harmonious order of being. But my parents objected, because this young man's parents were politically engaged, his father, Sean Mulready, had lost his job as a teacher for being a communist; he was subjected to a vilification campaign in the Catholic press. Fate sometimes appears to conspire in relation to the threads of our destiny, at the time I met this young man, I was working as an executive assistant in the Agricultural Institute in Dublin—an organization which had been endowed by the generous Marshall plan for Europe—and to my dismay, the new agricultural trends were for pouring fertilizer and chemicals into the earth—which was the subject of a very important book I read at the time, *Silent Spring* by Rachel Carson. The attachment to this young man, Seamus, and my reading of the book, propelled me into resigning from my job and taking the boat to England, where Seamus enrolled as a student in Birmingham, to support me and our putative children as an electrical engineer.

So this journey from innocence to experience was a painful one for me. I had been brought up a Catholic, with very poor knowledge of what were called the facts of life. Soon I was plunged into the maelstrom of political debate, from the very centre of the debate between communism and capitalism. Indeed Marx and Engels had written their principal work based on their experience of English cities which had suffered the industrial revolution. A century later, we were awash with consumerism, as cold war politics advanced unbridled spending on unnatural artifacts so that the war would be won for capitalism. I who had grown up in a household where not even a match was wasted, now found myself adrift in a town full of factories manufacturing ephemerals, throw-aways, and innumerable items—the more disposable, the more lauded.

It is easier for a woman writer to posit a state of innocence because women did not, as a rule, make up history. I imagined I was separate from this history of industrialization and consumption; after all, I had grown up without it. So it was possible for me to imagine the real Eden had been on earth and that man had been despoiler, since all who had brought about this state of affairs had been male. One of the first books I read in exile was *The Second Sex* by Simone de Beauvoir, but again, she had come from a wealthy middle class and shared some features of the fallen state of mankind and womankind. I needed to go back further. After evidence for the worship of the Great Goddess had come into the culture and we became aware of an age stretching back before recorded history, which had been unpolluted, we could say that the male sex had taken the role of exploiter/explorer, and when the initial haze of romance with Seamus had worn off, this became my understanding of the polluted state the world was in, as amply evidenced in Birmingham. For the first time I saw dirty rivers, and abandoned, rusty buildings, and ruined landscapes.

The poems in my second collection, which wasn't published until two decades later, has this despoliation of the landscape as its central theme. I focused on the sea, as I traveled the Irish Sea over and over during my exile, and became aware of the detritus and spillage from industrial pollution on what once James Joyce had called "ineluctable modality of the visible". What was visible now, unfortunately, was not beautiful, but spoiled. The nuclear power station, Windscale, later called Sellafield, had been built on the English coast at Cumbria during the 'fifties and I discovered that, following an accident there, in 1957, some radioactive material had been carried in the wind across to Dundalk, in Ireland, affecting schoolgirls, so that when they came to have their children in the next decade, there was a much higher incidence of birth defects.

The Thrust

The Sea is considered feminine. Rape is
The crime where the victim is not named:
Encrusted jewel flawed by hideous temerity
Pearl-theft sanctioned by fanatic greed
Issue praised. . . . .
And child a word for issue, when the child
Is beggared on a loving gentle spirit,
A throwaway thrust that reduces the sea
To a squandered dominion like an old tin can
Rusting in the waves, a raddled plangent queen
Whose health and beauty he did not esteem.

Science was man-centered, and man created. There was little room for women, there. The Great Goddess had left no writings behind, and any vestiges of her were hidden in the arcane traditions that were buried underground in the great cultural and materialist expansion of the Western world and its values. I imagined that perhaps she had left a note or message on a sea-shell. Just as I once and others before me had walked on an unpolluted shore.

Scratched on a Sea Shell

Once he possessed her in the yellow plain
A field of corn gave her the first madrigal
And she wrote with green reeds the alien rain
With nature, understanding, and grew magical
Child and garden..
But he had spoiled it, with her lost infinity.

That lost infinity has become the subject of much writing in the last thirty years, as women tried to find the self they would have been and lived through without male oppression

In remembering the silencing of the Great Goddess, perhaps the worst affront of patriarchy was the wars and dehumanization which had occurred, even in our lifetimes. There were huge questions to be resolved as well as feminist ones, such as what had happened during World War II. and the millions who had died. Theodore Adorno had written that no poetry was possible after Auschwitz

The Unremembered Tree

Across the dire straits of unremember
I flagged the ancient dower to grieve
With the raddled spirit of the sea
The golden pledge which the world can thieve
From the still leaves of an unremembered tree—
. . . .
Yet hills called back to Wordsworth, a wonder
To child, and a child to wonder.
Dachau, Hiroshima, the apostasy to sense
Where is that sweet vow, that inheritance?

Men had been in charge of the world when dreadful events like the Holocaust and the bombing of Hiroshima had taken place. Some women felt it was time they were given a chance. They might even do better, were they given the reins of power and the means to have their say. Throughout history, they had been silenced, and now we wanted to hear what their story was

In Ireland, we went about the usual way, making the mistakes of other countries without learning from our own experience. Rachel Carson's book lay in the library gathering dust, while the scientists of rural economy wrote their theses on soil and the need for nitrates, fertilizers, and the newest chemicals available to promote growth. I had resigned from my post, but my actions had no effect in the wider world. Our great grey mother, the sea, once boundless and seemingly infinite, now bore the marks of man's activity, like a spoiled and abused woman. It seemed man's sexual voracity, and indifference to female reactions to conserve and keep, was inherent However, it only seemed so, I had the example of my father to prove it was not a universal occurrence. It was the legacy of power and wealth which came down to us through history and most affected those born in our era.

Environmental destruction has been with us ever since the Second World War. My progress in life seemed to parallel the gradual despoliation of the natural world. Born in the year DDT was first concocted, I did not realize it would take about fifty years to win people away from the idea of scientific progress that believed the earth could be abused and life would not be affected.

There are still in our culture indications that we are not learning sufficiently fast about pollution. Nowadays, breast cancer is endemic in young women, the sight of a bald woman and an absent breast is becoming commonplace. There have been a few studies linking the widespread use of fertilizers and the occurrence of cancers in women and men, but if they would not listen to Rachel Carson, one wonders how much longer it will take for the obvious conclusions to be drawn, that the rise of cancer after World War II and the chemicals released into the food chain and sent up into the air from car exhausts are having an effect on health, the more so because the soft tissues have no way of expelling pollutants.

We are living through an uncontrolled experiment, where thousands of chemicals have been released into the environment and which must be affecting our health. Soft tissues store foreign substances that cannot easily be dislodged, so women and children are the ones most affected, though men suffer too from increasing sterility patterns, such as low sperm count.

As I found myself contemplating these matters in an industrial city mid-century, and preparing those poems which would tell the story of our modern affliction, Seamus, the man I was engaged to, discounted the idea that there was any link between the way nature was treated and the way women were treated. Perhaps because of being born in Ireland, and perhaps born before my time, I found most of the men I encountered were uncritical of the idea of unlimited scientific progress and consequently they ignored Nature and what was being done to the earth.

This first relationship with had taken place against a background of binary opposites, I was a Catholic, he was a Marxist, he was male, I was female, he was a materialist, I was spiritual. It struck me that this was the way history had happened, that man, as explorer and exploiter, told the story. It was time women told theirs, and their centuries old silence was broken.

The Pearl

He taught her to listen to herself. He was indifferent
To the schooled hearts of sealed wonder, who were stopped
In the anchor of discovery. So, seeing affection
Bold in her face, he trifled with her sex and lopped
Her head off. Language was unused to these themes
So she rested with the memory of her true lover
As she knelt on the shore of broken promises and dreams
Naked in the sand, where she could find no cover

What had started as an act of bold self assertion, my leaving my home, family and job for a wider view, led to a minefield in my personal life, which seemed all about politics. At school, we had no idea of the Enlightenment, with its anthropocentric world view. Instead we were taught to argue against evolution, and against scientific materialism. This was a good training in a way, especially for the mind, but students like myself, of this sort of philosophy were ill prepared for life's challenges in the new world which grew up after World War II, with its emphasis on progress, particularly materialist progress.

I was drawn to the relationship which challenged me most, however it turned out to be ultimately destructive. It took many years to disentangle myself. Seamus may have had the questions, but he had not the answers either. He held that the new Marxist states were the shape of the future. Their denial of selfhood and their abuse of personal rights was endemic in the philosophy, as their view of scientific determinism, first advanced by Hegel, and then developed by Marx, meant they did not believe in personal relationships, or in love other than a vast abstract duty to mankind in general...

Marx was not an advocate of women's rights, though he believed in the freedom of the individual under the banner of equality. However, in practice, Marx allowed his daughter to die rather than have medical treatment which would have cost him too much. Engels was disposed towards women's rights when he wrote *The Origin of the Family*, as he believed that the suppression of women was a result of capitalism, and when capitalism was overthrown, women would be freed as well. His experiences in the textile factories of Manchester at the age of 22 marked him for life, as it did anyone who worked there.

However, Marxism in practice, by putting objective consciousness forward as the pinnacle of truth has led to a dehumanization in effect, and because men had been the chief arbiters of this kind of scientific discourse, men were given an extra armory to abuse women. Some feminists in the seventies took up Marxist philosophy to describe their own state of colonization at the hands of men. Marxism again asked the questions, but did not give us the answers. Women were still being seen either as essentialist, or as victims of colonialism which came to be called patriarchy. However the link between woman and nature was broken by the Marxists, as they denied subjectivity, and consequently the appreciation of natural forms and beauty—women were seen as primarily material beings with the wrong socialization. The family was under attack, in many cases rightly so, for oppressing women. But my father had not oppressed me, as he had gone out to work to give his entire family including the girls an education. He had Hollywood good looks, and a wonderful intelligence. He had quit school to support his mother, a widow, and then he went on to support us, daughters as well as sons. Therefore the he who oppressed was not a universal he, but an historical occurrence in some cultures.

The Marxist discourse was materialist, and pseudo-scientific, and therefore anti-Nature. Just as objective reality denied the spiritual, I found that the spirit had answered back to the demands of matter.

Her Story

His word set a tombstone on my heart
Impelled the knife's silhouette into my side
The brown speck on his eye was a part
Of beauty's fungus, a leprosy of pride
Still in the whited paling of my soul
I let this dark transparency take root
To drive into the earth of my whole
Spring, fantasy's festering shoot.

Marxism denied the individual and the spiritual in a very hostile way. Matter which was then thought of as inert, powerful, and dense (it took some years for news of particle physics to reach Birmingham). This matter was held to control life itself. And woman was supreme matter, wasn't the very word, mother, mater in Latin, resonant of matter? The whole succession of events since the beginning of the world could be explained away as the determinism of matter. According to Professor George Thomson, one of Seamus's friends whom I met in Birmingham, the speech of mankind (note mankind) was a conditioned reflex, having its origin in the grunts of labor gangs, the first form of organized society. However, Professor Thomson held original views on Greek drama in the pre-Hellenic period, but like most Marxists held to the strictly materialist interpretation of the world. According to this school of thought, philosophy and poetry were merely the products of a leisured class in a society. The entire canon of Western society rested on the fact that a slave caste had done all the hard work, freeing philosophers and scribes to talk about freedom and the ideals of society, freedoms which were denied to the workers or slaves, or women. This defect in western philosophy, the absence of the feminine, and of the worker, vitiated its content and many feminists later came to think the whole of western philosophy was invalid, and written by DWEMs, dead white European males. As I struggled alone in Birmingham in the pre-feminist era, battling materialism and crude objectivity, I found myself isolated, and indeed, afflicted. Some people have found my book *The Sea of Affliction*[1] too painful, but it was my experience that many people, especially women, felt like me, and were unable to articulate it until later. It was quite an undertaking to question the whole canon of European thought, and it needed the sisterhood, yet to emerge, to give it context and meaning.

There were some fierce arguments about form and content, and Seamus and the Marxists held the view that style and wit were essentially decorative, therefore not intrinsic, and because of this, were corrupt. As an extension of materialist masculinity, woman's form was inferior in function to man's, and should be dressed down, preferably with hair cut off, in order that the formal attributes of the woman be not emphasized at the cost of her material functions, that is her aspiration to equality. This kind of thinking has led to women becoming male surrogates in the workforce. However, a crude kind of essentialism prevailed in our discourse, since I was irreducibly feminine, and amid the torrents of words that we flung at each other there was always an undercurrent that the woman was not as good as the man, indeed should be subject to him, in other words, be an object to him, and to herself. Being an object to myself was difficult, and at this time, the Cultural Revolution in China was at its height. People's subjective experiences were not only invalid there, but criminal. China was going through this retrograde reformation at the same time as I experienced the denial of self, the denial of personhood, and the denial of love. The "I" was looked upon as a false construct, and the subterranean emotions beneath as mere mechanics: what was called "false consciousness".

Even when religion was mentioned as the villain, and as the opium of the people, it still didn't tally with my earlier, idyllic experiences. The Marxist idea that all ornamentation was corrupt and belonged to the aristocracy was questioned at root in our home. I wondered, thinking of Irish music, and how the materially poor musicians I had grown up with had the most wonderful flourishes and grace notes. Seamus and his friends found people from the West in Ireland difficult to pigeonhole and categorize, so we were a real threat. The abuse followed.

So, in some respects, I did not have the usual feminist discontent with all of the male sex as my father had encouraged me to write. Much later on, I found a concerted appeal with the small group of women achievers who had been encouraged by their fathers, such as Hannah Arendt, Simone Weil, and Artemisia Gentileschi, who had achieved greatness in philosophy and art long before the second wave of feminism.

I didn't expect to be a victim of a Marxist exploiter, but such a grip the philosophy had on his—and my imagination that I stayed with him to end the argument, as I thought, but after an enforced pregnancy, and a miscarriage, began to feel again the extraordinary passivity of women in face of the facts of birth, life, and death. In a way, we were more like Nature, having cycles of fertility, growth, and death, just like the trees, the grass, and even the stars grow and wax strong and then fade some becoming supernovae and ending in a death in the cosmos. But I realized that to think this way was to opt out of personal responsibility. Yet it was the philosophic basis of choosing activism, but the activism was in response to the false philosophy. This was a paradox at the heart of the green movement, but I felt a Nietzschean imperative to act, as he believed we should act out our ideas.

Strange as it may seem, it was the jargon that hurt the most, and it had a strange effect on me. When Seamus spoke of the imperialism of nations, it struck me at once that women were objects of colonialism in the same way that countries were. When he talked of exploitation, I thought of nature and resources being used with no responsibility to society or to the future, and it struck me also as a paradigm for how history had treated women. I reluctantly had to recognize that there was a correspondence at work, that just as he spoke of nature being polluted I found this essentially was the way I was being treated, and how women were treated down the centuries.

This man, Seamus, who explained exploration and colonialism as automatic history, could not see the parallels. He was treating me badly in a personal relationship, even to the point where the person and individual was denied. As he talked about the abuse of nature, he abused me. I ended up feeling like nature, some natural resource that was littered, sprayed with pesticide, fungicide, force fed with strange chemicals, with no right of reply. I who had once aspired to write was now mere object, and the paradigm of virtue was now corrupted by an alien presence, man himself, incarnate and superior in the natural order. I began to suspect there was more to this than sexism.

However, the effects of this abusive relationship were that I suffered for many years afterwards. It had happened when I was isolated from my family. As a student teacher in Birmingham, I woke to dismay each morning as the sound of boots came to me from my window. From my curtains at seven in the morning, I could see hordes of people scurrying in the dark looking neither up nor down, but moving rigidly and painfully into the grey surroundings of factories. I had the luxury of not being due into school until nine o'clock. I thought of my good job in Ireland, how I had left the Agricultural Institute, worried about the land, only to find myself in the middle of an industrial town where the inhabitants had scarcely breathed fresh air from the day they were born. Their ancestors had been dragged from the countryside and shoved into plants and mills, Blake's "dark satanic mills".

More than a reminder of the repugnance of chemically treated earth, the people of Birmingham stayed with me. More than anything else, they resembled matter—they were starved of the spiritual, and it was a painful realization. Some puppet master had decreed their blind eye, their mechanical gait, their slumped shoulders, and their sense of desperation that existed for them more than any life they could have chosen. They were the direct heirs of the Industrial Revolution, of materialist progress, and of scientific materialism, and how they were stunted. Their only outlet was the sensationalist, tabloid press, which paid scant attention to environmental issues. One could argue that they had been determined by their environment, were it not for the fact of their deep suffering which was so apparent. No wonder Engels wanted to rescue them.

However, I could find little comfort in books at the time. The crisis in industrial society was far advanced. Some writers had been prophetic about this development, but Blake was dismissed by my contemporaries as mad. The whole of life resembled a test tube, life itself was being experimented on and it had to answer back. I would scavenge desperately for a ray of light, a crumb of comfort, a hope. I turned back to Ireland to salvage my identity, and had started publishing poetry.

My first effort was called "Nightmare in three parts"—being an individual woman in a mechanized society was a nightmare for me. It was published in the college literary magazine in 1967, and my career as a writer began.

At that time, when I started publishing poetry, it was seen as an act of defiance against the established order. One critic, Geoffrey Thurley, who has since written standard academic works, wrote that I was "100% improvement on Christina Rossetti"! The effect of publishing verse was extraordinary. Seamus, the man I was engaged to, reacted with panic and dismay, lost his head, involving me in a hasty marriage He ended up trying to commit suicide. Clearly I had hit upon a nerve. I took him to the hospital and made up my mind to leave this state of emotional blackmail. Once his life was secure, I abandoned him until another ministering angel moved in to look after him, but what about me? My family would not speak to me because I had married in a registry office. There was no divorce in Ireland. I was ineligible overnight for teaching or working in the Civil Service, to which my college course of Arts in English, Irish and philosophy was directed. Most women I knew were already deciding to live in the suburbs and give up all hopes of a career. Feminist battles lay ahead, but at the time I was atypical

I was female, and Irish, and I went to Trinity College which had been the bastion of British imperialism in Ireland. I tried to find a *modus vivendi* in this place with values that were the antithesis to those I had been brought up with. The priest thundered from the pulpit that a Catholic who went to Trinity was doomed to hell.

I looked to my contemporaries, young men and women, for a way out. It was the hippy era, and there was a golden dawn of optimism. However, some of my fellow students embodied the very class notions I had been struggling against—the deterministic, typecast bourgeois so detested by the Irish left wing. What had distinguished them was a hauteur that they would gradually cast aside deliberately in order to court the notion of equality. It occurred to me that the same blind egoism which lies in a private domain was at work here whereas I and my notions of identity had undergone a sustained assault whilst in industrialized Birmingham. This blind egoism lay behind the opaque constructs of those who promoted waste in the Cold War in order to win the battle for freedom in the west. The individual was accented, and greed became the norm. It began to seem normal to be greedy, and to sacrifice principle to a result, a reduction which meant that the truth lay broken like a corncrake's nest under the tractor. The small farm gave way to factory farming, and despite Rachel Carson's warnings, the bird population began to disappear. The incidence of cancer in young people began to rise. What was a newsworthy story, a young person getting cancer, now was a commonplace of children's wards in hospitals. Legions of bald young men took the place of the sixties hippies with their long hair and fertile locks.

In my peer group there were very few men who encouraged women to write, or to excel in any public role. This was changed later on by the advent of women's rights in Ireland in the seventies and eighties, culminating in the election of the first Irish woman President, Mary Robinson in 1990.

However, during the sixties, as a young woman, what puzzled me was the way I was treated. I did not believe in the essentialist view that woman existed to be a sexual toy for men and a procreator of children, that she was biologically determined. However things were against me because of my gender, the law clearly discriminated against me because of my sex, since I was legally barred from work as a teacher or a civil servant. The legislation would be amended in time, but in the meantime I was in a tough situation.

Bad Faith

It happened to me, too. I left the road
Of jewel-encrusted happiness for your lie
Because that explained the misery of the world.
. . . .
Bread went stale in my house, the birds left
For aromatic gardens hung between
Time and space and our great year of doubt.
Their fragrance came to me in the ship's cabin
Where I was logging your philosophy as dementia praecox
I plundered mythologies, the tree and cross were banned.
All this for one lie! But it poisoned me.
It pursued me like a golden serpent
And turned to dust the memory of our youth.

The mechanisms of journalism, the consumption of experience, first noticed in the sixties, and the restructuring of the "I" around empirical values now found its way into poetry. Poetry in general began to resemble a form of telegraphese.

I took refuge in form, as I had tried to find refuge in music, embracing form as a spiritual quest. I found a quatrain by Richard Lovelace which encapsulated the way that among the strictures of form I had found a freeing force in me.

To Althea, from Prison

When I lye tangled in her haire,
And fetterd to her eye,
The birds, that wanton in the aire,
Know no such liberty.

I wrote *Flight into Reality* a long poem in terza rima, based on a spiritual quest for love, to throw off the shackles of materialism and embrace beauty and form such as existed in Nature. Somewhere in England the wheels were turning. As time passed, hope became possible. I took part in green activities, and continued to write. Kathleen Raine, the eminent poet and scholar, came to Ireland to read her poetry and talk of spiritual tradition. I met her in Dublin during an arts festival, and she invited me to contribute to her journal, *Temenos*, where a sacred space was created for the imagination right in the place where the Enlightenment began and where science began its ascent. In *Temenos*, science received its measure as a secondary principle, Nature was first.

She dared mention the soul, she was benign to the cause of spirit. She saw the forms of nature and celebrated its magnificent treasury. Another great spirit began to sweeten the earth and lift up our hearts with hope.

My love of nature was restored to me, as I found others who shared my quest in our most materialist of ages, to rescue nature and the spiritual from the trappings of pollution and waste.

Notes

1. *The Sea of Affliction* can be downloaded free under a Creative Commons agreement which requests that author and publisher be credited if material is used. The website address is: http://www.irishliteraryrevival.com/rosemarierowley.html. Some of the poems in this essay were originally published in *The Sea of Affliction*.

Bibliography

Abram, David. "Turning Inside Out." *Orion* 15, no. 1 (1996): 54-58.

Ackerman, Jennifer. *Notes From the Shore.* New York: Penguin Books, 1995.

Adams, Carol J. "Feminist Traffic in Animals." *Ecofeminism: Women, Animals, Nature.* Greta Gaard, ed. Philadelphia: Temple University Press, 1993. 195-218.

Alaimo, Stacy. "Cyborg and Ecofeminist Interventions: Challenges for an Environmental Feminism." *Feminist Studies* 20, no. 1 (1994): 133-152.

———. *Undomesticated Ground: Recasting Nature as Feminist Space.* Ithaca, NY: Cornell University Press, 2000.

Alter, Robert. *Genesis: Translation and Commentary.* New York: W. W. Norton, 1996.

Anzaldúa, Gloria. *Borderlands/La Frontera: The New Mestiza.* San Fransisco: Aunt Lute Books, 1987.

Anzaldúa, Gloria, and Cherrie Moraga, eds. *This Bridge Called My Back: Writings by Radical Women of Color.* Waterton, MA: Persephone Press, 1981.

Arrendondo, Gabriela, Aida Hurtado et al., eds. *Chicana Feminisms.* Durham, NC: Duke University Press, 2003.

Atwood, Margaret. *Eating Fire: Selected Poetry 1965-1995.* London: Virago, 1998.

———. *Oryx and Crake.* London: Virago, 2004.

———. "A Reply." *Sign: Journal of Women in Culture and Society* 2, no. 2 (1976): 340-341.

———. *Surfacing* .London: Virago, 1979.

———. *Wilderness Tips*, 3d ed. London: Virago, 1997.

Austin, Mary. *The Land of Journey's Ending.* New York: The Century Co., 1924.

Bachelard, Gaston. *The Poetics of Space.* Boston: Beacon Press, 1964, 1994.

Beran, Carol L. "Strangers within the Gates: Margaret Atwood's *Wilderness Tips.*" In *Margaret Atwood's Textual Assassinations: Recent Poetry and Fiction.* Sharon Rose Wilson, ed. Columbus: The Ohio University State Press, 2003, 74-87.

Berleant, Arnold. *The Aesthetics of Environment.* Philadelphia: Temple Univesity Press, 1992.

Birke, Lynda. *Feminism, Animals, Science: The Naming of the Shrew.* Buckham: Open University Press, 1994.

Birkeland, Janis. "Ecofeminism: Linking Theory and Practice." In *Ecofeminism: Women, Animals, Nature*. Greta Gaard, ed. Philadelphia: Temple University Press, 1993.

Blend, Benay. "Intersections of Nature and the Self in Chicana Writing." In *New Essays in Ecofeminist Literary Critcism*. Glynis Carr, ed. Lewisburg: Bucknell University Press, 2000.

Brady, Mary Pat. *Extinct Lands, Temporal Geographies: Chicana Literature and the Urgency of Space*. Durham, NC: Duke University Press, 2002.

Braidotti, Rosi, Ewa Charkiewicz et al., eds. *Women, the Environment, and Sustainable Development: Towards a Theoretical Synthesis*. Atlantic Highlands, NJ: Zed Books, 1994.

Buckles, Mary Parker. *A Naturalist Meets the Long Island Sound*. New York: Farrar, Strauss and Giroux, 1997.

Butler, Octavia E. *Parable of the Sower*. New York: Aspect Press, 1993.

——. *Parable of the Talents*. New York: Aspect, 1998.

Carby, Hazel. "Figuring the Future in Los(t) Angeles." *Comparative American Studies* 1 (2003):19-34.

Carson, Rachel. *The Edge of the Sea*. New York: Signet Books, 1955.

———. *The Sea Around Us*. New York: Oxford University Press, 1950, 1989.

———. *Silent Spring*. Boston: Houghton Mifflin, 1962, 1987.

Casey, Edward. "Body, Self, and Landscape: A Geo-philosophical Inquiry into the Place World." In *Textures of Place: Exploring Humanist Geographies*. Paul Adams, ed. Minneapolis: University of Minnesota Press, 2001.

Cather, Willa. *Death Comes for the Archbishop*. New York: Vintage, 1990.

Chi, Lu. "Rhymeprose on Literature." Achilles Fang, trans. *The New Directions Anthology of Classical Chinese Poetry*. New York: New Directions, 2003.

Christ, Carol P. "Margaret Atwood: The Surfacing of Women's Spiritual Quest and Vision." *Sign: Journal of Women in Culture and Society* 2, no. 2 (1976): 316-330.

Cixous, Helene. "The Laugh of the Medusa." Keith Cohen and Paula Cohen, trans. *Signs* 1 (1976): 875-93.

——. "Sorties Out and Out: Attacks/Ways Out/Forays." In *The Logic of the Gift: Toward an Ethic of Generosity*. Alan D. Schrift, ed. New York and London: Routledge, 1997, 148-173.

Collins, Patricia Hill. "The Meaning of Motherhood in Black Culture and Black Mother-Daughter Relationships." In *Double Stitch: Black Women Write About Mothers and Daughters*. Patricia Bell-Scott and Beverley Guy-Sheftall, eds. New York: Harper-Perennial Press, 1993, 42-60.

Corbin, Alice. *Red Earth: Poems of New Mexico*. Santa Fe: Museum of New Mexico Press, 2003.

Cronon, William. "The Trouble with Wilderness: or, Getting Back to the Wrong Nature." In *Uncommon Ground: Rethinking the Human Place in Nature*. William Cronon, ed. New York: Norton, 1996, 69-90.

Cuomo, Chris J. *Feminism and Ecological Communities*. New York: Routledge, 1998.

Daly, Mary *Gyn/Ecology: The Metaethics of Radical Feminism*. Boston: Beacon, 1990.

d'Eaubonne, Françoise "What Could an Eco-Feminist Society Be?" *Liberty, Equality and Women?* Jacob Paisain, trans. *Ethics and the Environment* 4, no. 2: 179-184.

de Beauvoir, Simone. *The Coming of Age*. New York: Putnam, 1972.

Deery, June. "Science for Feminists: Margaret Atwood's Body of Knowledge." *Twentieth Century Literature* 43, no. 4 (1994).

Diamond, Irene, and Gloria Feman Orenstien, eds. *Reweaving the World: The Emergence of Ecofeminism.* San Francisco: Sierra Books, 1990.

Dillard, Annie. *Pilgrim at Tinker Creek.* New York: Harper's Magazine Press, 1974.

Donovan, Josephine. "Animal Rights and Feminist Theory." *Ecofeminism: Women, Animals, Nature.* Greta Gaard, ed. Philadelphia: Temple University Press, 1993, 167-96.

Dubey, Madhu. "Folk and Urban Communities in African-American Women's Fiction: Octavia Butler's *Parable of the Sower.*" *Studies in American Fiction* 27 (March, 1999): 1, 103-28

Eichstaedt, Peter H. *If You Poison Us: Uranium and Native Americans.* Santa Fe: Red Crane Books, 1994.

Engels, Frederick. *The Origin of the Family, Private Property and the State.* Introduction by Evelyn Reed. New York, Pathfinder, 1973.

Escoda, Clara. "The Relationship Between Community and Subjectivity in Octavia E. Butler's *Parable of the Sower.*" *Extrapolation* 46 (2005): 3, 351-359.

Fewkes, J. W. *A Journal of Ethnology and Archaeology, Vol IV.* Ann Arbor, MI: Xerox University Microfilms, 1976.

Gaard, Greta, ed. *Ecofeminism: Women, Animals, Nature.* Philadelphia: Temple University Press, 1993.

Gatens, Moira. "Power, Bodies and Difference." *Destabilizing Theory.* Michele Barrett and Anne Phillips, eds. Stanford, CA: Stanford University Press, 1992.

Gimbutas, Marija. *The Language of the Goddess.* San Francisco: HarperCollins, 1991.

Glotfelty, Cheryll. "Introduction: Literary Studies in an Age of Environmental Crisis." *The Ecocriticism Reader.* Cheryll Glotfelty and Harold Fromm, eds. Athens: University of Georgia Press, 1996, xv-xxxvii.

Gluck, Louise. "The Egg." *Firstborn The First Four Books of Poems.* New Jersey: Ecco Press, 1968, 1995.

——. *Proofs & Theories.* New Jersey: Ecco Press, 1994.

Goldstick, Miles, and John Graham, eds. *Voices from Wollaston Lake—An Account of the Campaign Against the Dumping of Nuclear Waste in Saskatchewan.* Canada: Earth Embassy/Wise, 1987.

Gordon, Maggie. "A Woman Writing about Nature: Louise Gluck and 'the absence of intention.'" In *Ecopoetry : A Critical Introduction.* J. Scott Bryson, ed. Salt Lake City: University of Utah Press, 2002.

Gutiérrez, Ramón. *When Jesus Came, The Corn Mothers Went Away: Marriage Sexuality, and Power in New Mexico, 1500-1846.* Stanford, CA: Stanford University Press, 1991.

Haraway, Donna. *Primate Visions: Gender, Race, and Nature in the World of Modern Science.* New York: Routledge, 1989.

Hampson, Daphne. *After Christianity.* London: SCM Press, 2002.

Hegland, Jean. *Into the Forest.* New York: Bantam Books Press, 1998.

Hertog, Susan. *Ann Morrow Lindbergh: Her Life.* New York: DoubleDay, 1999.

Hirshfield, Jane. *Nine Gates: Entering the Mind of Poetry.* New York: Harper, 1997.

Hoda, Zaki. "Utopia, Dystopia, and Ideology in the Science Fiction of Octavia Butler." *Science Fiction Studies* 17 (1990): 239-251.

Holy Bible, The. King James Version. Rev. C. I. Scofield, ed. New York: Oxford University Press, 1945: John 1:1.

Homans, Margaret. *Bearing the Word: Language and Female Experience in Nineteenth-Century Women's Writing*. Chicago: University of Chicago Press, 1986.

hooks, bell. "Revolutionary Parenting." In *Feminist Theory: From Margin to Center*. Boston: South End Press, 1990, 41-49.

Ingersoll, Earl E. "Survival in Margaret Atwood's Novel *Oryx and Crake*." *Extrapolation* 45, no. 2 (2004): 162- 176.

Irigaray, Luce. "Cosi Fan Tutti." *The Sex Which is Not One*. Catherine Porter and Carolyn Burke, trans. Ithaca, NY: Cornell University Press, 1985.

———. "The 'Mechanics' of Fluids." *This Sex Which is Not One*. Catherine Porter and Carolyn Burke, trans. Ithaca, NY: Cornell University Press, 1985.

Joyce, James. *Ulysses*. Paris: Sylvia Beach, 1922.

Keating, AnaLouise, ed. *Interviews/Entrevistas*. New York: Routledge, 2000.

Kelly, Walt. *Pogo: We Have Met the Enemy and He Is Us*. New York: Simon Schuster, 1972.

Kheel, Marti. "From Heroic to Holistic Ethics: The Ecofeminist Challenge." *Ecofeminism: Women, Animals, Nature*. Greta Gaard, ed. Philadelphia: Temple University Press, 1993. 243-271.

Kittany, Eva Feder. "Woman as Metaphor." *Feminist Social Thought*. Diana Tietjens Meyers, ed. New York and London: Routledge, 1997.

Kolodny, Annette. *The Land Before Her: Fantasy and Experience of the American Frontiers, 1630-1860*. Chapel Hill: University of North Carolina Press, 1984.

Krafel, Paul. *Seeing Nature: Deliberate Encounters with the Visible World*. White River Junction, VT: Chelsea Green, 1999.

Lamott, Anne. *Bird by Bird: Some Instructions on Writing and Life*. New York: Anchor Books, 1995.

Lear, Linda. "Life and Legacy of Rachel Carson." Rachel Carson Home Page. 1998. http://www.rachelcarson.org.

——. *Rachel Carson: Witness for Nature*. New York: Henry Holt and Company, 1997.

LeGuin, Ursula K. "The Carrier Bag Theory of Fiction." In *The Ecocriticism Reader*. Cheryll Glotfelty and Harold Fromm, eds. Athens: University of Georgia Press, 1996, 149-154.

Leopold, Aldo. *The Sand County Almanac*. New York: Ballantine Books, 1949, 1970.

Lindbergh, Anne Morrow. *Gift from the Sea*. New York: Pantheon Books, 1955, 1997.

Luhan, Mabel Dodge. *Edge of Taos Desert: An Escape to Reality*. Albuquerque: University of New Mexico Press, 1987.

———. *Taos Winter*. Santa Fe: Las Palomas De Taos, 1983.

Lummis, Charles F. *Some Strange Corners of Our Country: The Wonderland of the Southwest*. Tucson: University of Arizona Press, 1989.

Maloof, Joan. *Teaching the Trees: Lessons from the Forest*. Athens: University of Georgia Press, 2005.

Manes, Christopher. "Nature and Silence." *The Ecocriticism Reader*. Cheryll Glotfelty and Harold Fromm, eds. Athens: University of Georgia Press, 1996, 15-29.

Marx, Karl, and Frederick Engels. *The Communist Manifesto*. Introduction by Chris Harman. London: Bookmarks, 2003.

Mayer, Sylvia. "Genre and Environmentalism: Octavia Butler's Parable of the Sower, Speculative Fiction, and the African American Slave Narrative." Sylvia Mayer, ed. *Restoring the Connection to the Natural World: Essays on the African American Environmental Imagination*. Münster, Germany: LIT Press, 2003, 175-196.

Melzer, Patricia. "'All That You Touch You Change': Utopian Desire and the Concept of Change in Octavia Butler's *Parable of the Sower* and *Parable of the Talents.*" *Femspec* 3 (2002): 31-52.

Merchant, Carolyn. *The Death of Nature: Women, Ecology and the Scientific Revolution.* San Francisco: Harper & Row, Publishers, 1983.

——. *Radical Ecology: The Search for a Livable World.* New York: Routledge, 2005.

——. *Reinventing Eden: The Fate of Nature in Western Culture.* New York: Routledge, 2004.

Miller, Jim, "Post-Apocalyptic Hoping: Octavia Butler's Dystopian Utopian Vision." *Science Fiction Studies* 25 (1988): 336-360.

Moore, Kathleen Dean. *Holdfast: At Home in the Natural World.* New York: Lyons Press, 1999.

——. *The Pine Island Paradox: Making Connections in a Disconnected World.* Minneapolis: Milkweed Press. 2004.

——. *Riverwalking: Reflections on Moving Water.* New York: Harcourt Brace & Company, 1995.

Nelson, Richard. *The Island Within.* New York: Vintage Books, 1989.

Noddings, Nel, and Paul J. Shore, eds. *Awakening the Inner Eye: Intuition in Education.* Troy, NY: Educator's International Press, 1998.

O'Reilly, Andrea. *Rocking the Cradle: Thoughts on Motherhood, Feminism and the Possibility of Empowered Mothering.* Toronto: Demeter Press, 2006.

Payne, Michael, ed. *Cultural and Critical Theory.* Oxford: Blackwell, 2001

Parra, Andrea. "Forum on Literatures of the Environment." *PMLA* 114 (Oct. 1999): 1099-1100.

Phillips, Dana. *The Truth of Ecology: Nature, Culture, and Literature in America.* Oxford: Oxford University Press, 2003.

Plaskow, Judith. "On Carol Christ on Margaret Atwood: Some Theological Re flections." *Sign: Journal of Women in Culture and Society* 2, no. 2 (1976): 331-339.

Plumwood, Val. *Feminism and the Mastery of Nature.* New York: Routledge, 1993.

Poole, Roger. *Towards Deep Subjectivity.* New York and London: Harper Torchbooks, 1972, 141, 142, 143, 145, quoted in Daphne Hampson, *After Christianity.* London: SCM Press, 2002.

Pyle, Robert Michael. *Walking the High Ridge: Life as a Field Trip.* Minneapolis: Milkweed Editions, 2000.

Robinson, Sally. "The 'Anti-Logos Weapon': Multiplicity in Women's Texts." *Contemporary Literature* 29, no. 1 (1988): 105-124.

Ross, Andrew. "Wet, Dark, and Low, Eco-Man Evolves from Eco-Woman." *Boundary* 2, 19, no. 2 (1992): 206- 217.

Rowley, Rosemarie. "Thinking Locally and Acting Globally." In *Across the Frontiers.* Richard Kearney, ed. Dublin: Wolfhound, Dublin, 1988.

Rudnick, Lois Palken. *Mabel Dodge Luhan: New Woman, New Worlds* Albuquerque: University of New Mexico Press, 1984.

Ruether, Rosemary Radford. "Ecofeminism: Symbolic and Social Connection of the Oppression of Women and the Domination of Nature." In *Ecofeminism and the Sacred.* Carol J. Robb, ed. New York: Crossroad Books, 1993, 13-23.

Sachs, Carolyn. *Gendered Fields: Rural Women, Agriculture, and Environment.* Boulder, CO: Westview Press, 1996.

Seager, Joni. "Rachel Carson Died of Breast Cancer: the Coming of Age of Feminist Environmentalism." *Signs* 28, no. 3 (Spring 2003): 945-74. Academic One File.

Anne Arundel Community College Lib., Arnold, MD. http://find.galegroup.com.ezproxy.aacc.edu (accessed March 31, 2007).

Schaefer, Heike. *Mary Austin's Regionalism: Reflections on Gender, Genre, and Geography.* Charlottesville: University of Virginia Press, 2004.

Schedler, Christopher. "Writing Culture: Willa Cather's Southwest." In *Willa Cather and the American Southwest.* John N. Swift and Joseph R. Urgo, eds. Lincoln: University of Nebraska, 2002, 108-123.

Scott, Joan W. "The Identity in Question." *October* 61 (Summer 1992): 108-120.

Shiga, David. "Parasitoid wasps use viruses as a weapon." *Science News* 167 (2005): 136-137.

Silko, Leslie Marmon. *Sacred Water.* Tucson: Flood Plain Press, 1993.

Silverman, Kaja. *The Threshold of the Visible World.* New York : Routledge, 1996.

Somma, Mark, and Sue Tolleson-Rinehart. "Tracking the Elusive Green: Sex, Environmentalism, and Feminism in the United States and Europe." *Politi- cal Research Quarterly* 50, no. 1 (1997), 153- 169.

Soper, Kate. *What is Nature?* Oxford: Blackwell Publishers, 1995.

Stafford, William. *The Way It Is: New and Selected Poems.* Saint Paul, MN: Graywolf Press, 1999.

Stillman, Peter B. "Dystopian Critiques, Utopian Possibilities, and Human Purposes in Octavia Butler's '*Parables*'." *Utopian Studies* 14 (2003): 1, 15-35.

Steele, Cassie Premo. *We Heal From Memory: Sexton, Lorde, Anzaldúa, and the Poetry of Witness.* New York: Palgrave, 2000.

Struckel, Katie. "The Human Nature of Margaret Atwood." *Reader's Digest* 80, no. 10 (2000): 35.

Suzuki, David, and Wayne Grady. *Tree: a Life Story.* Vancouver: Greystone Books, 2004.

Sydee, Jasmin, and Sharon Beder. *Democracy and Nature.* July (2001): 281-302.

Thompson, Charis. "Back to Nature? Resurrecting Ecofeminism After Poststructuralist and Third-wave Feminisms." *Isis* 97, no. 3 (Sept 2006): 505-513. Academic One File. Anne Arundel Community College Lib., Arnold, MD. http://find.galegroup.com.ezproxy.aacc.edu (accessed March 31, 2007).

Thomson, George. *Aeschylus and Athens, A Study in the Social Origins of Drama.* 3rd ed. London: Lawrence and Wishart, 1967.

——. *From Marx to Mao Tse-tung—a Study in Revolutionary Dialectics.* London: China Policy Study Group, 1971.

——. *Marxism andPoetry.* London: Lawrence and Wishart, 1975.

——. *Studies in Ancient Greek Society: The First Philosophers.* London: Lawrence and Wishart, 1977.

Thoreau, Henry David. "The Succession of Forest Trees." In *Natural History Essays.* Salt Lake City: Peregrine Smith Books, reprint edition, 1989.

Tong, Rosemarie. *Feminist Thought.* 2nd ed. Boulder, CO: Westview Press, 1998.

Tyler, Hamilton A. *Pueblo Gods and Myths.* Norman: University of Oklahoma Press, 1964.

Upton, Lee. "Fleshless Voices: Louise Gluck's Rituals of Abjection and Oblivion." In *The Muse of Abandonment: Origin, Identity, Mastery in Five American Poets.* Lewisburg: Bucknell University Press, 1998.

Warren, Karen J. "Taking Empirical Data Seriously: An Ecofeminist Philosophical Perspective," In *Ecofeminism: Women, Culture, Nature*. Bloomington: Indiana University Press, 1997, 3-20.

Williams, Terry Tempest. *Red: Passion and Patience in the Desert*. New York: Random House, 2001.

——. *Refuge: An Unnatural History of Family and Place*. New York: Vintage Books, 1991.

Wilson, E. O. *Biophilia*. Cambridge, MA: Harvard University Press, 1984.

Zwinger, Susan. *The Last Wild Edge: One Woman's Journey from the Arctic Circle to the Olympic Rain Forest*. Colorado: Johnson Books, 1999.

——. *Stalking the Ice Dragon: An Alaskan Journey*. Tucson: University of Arizona Press, 1991.

Index

About the Contributors

Mary Kate Azcuy is lecturer of English at Monmouth University. Her current research involves American poet Louise Gluck and poet and fiction writer Leslie Marmon Silko. She is a published poet and lives in Monmouth County, New Jersey.

Barbara J. Cook is assistant professor at Mount Aloysius College in Pennsylvania where she teaches Native American literature, literature and the environment, and other American literature courses. She edited the collection *From the Center of Tradition: Critical Perspectives on Linda Hogan* which was the co-winner of the 2003 Colorado Endowment for the Humanities Publications Prize. Her articles have appeared in the *Northwest Review, Southwest American Literature,* and *American Indian Quarterly*.

H. Louise Davis is a Ph.D. Candidate in American Studies at Michigan State University. Her most recent publications include book chapters in *War Bodies on Scree*n, *Women in Rock*, and *Mothering and Popular Culture* .

Alex Hunt is assistant professor of American literature and American studies at West Texas A&M University. Specializing in Western American literature and ecocriticism, he has published articles on Cormac McCarthy, Leslie Marmon Silko, Rudolfo Anaya, the U.S./Mexico border, and nature writing.

Heidi Hutner, associate professor of English at SUNY Stony Brook, is the author of *Colonial Women* and the editor of *Rereading Aphra Behn: History, Theory, Criticism.* She has written numerous articles on eighteenth-century women writers. Her current book project is entitled, *Ecofeminism and Mothering in Contemporary American Literature and Film.*

Joan E. Maloof is the author of *Teaching the Trees: Lessons from the Forest.* She has essays published in numerous places, including *Writing the Future:*

Progress and Evolution; *Interdisciplinary Studies in Literature and Environment; Earthlight;* and *New Scientist.* She has a Ph.D. in ecology from the University of Maryland and teaches biological sciences and environmental Issues at Salisbury University. She may be contacted at jemaloof@salisbury.edu.

Sarah E. McFarland is assistant professor of English at Northwestern State University of Louisiana. She is interested in how agency, subjectivity, and power are articulated in nonfiction literature and film about other animals. She has published articles about Barry Lopez and Terry Tempest Williams and is working on a book project about representations of animals in American nature writing.

Susan A. C. Rosen, earned her MA and Ph.D. in literature from the University of Maryland, College Park. She is the editor of. *Shorewords: A Collection of American Coastal Women's Writings.* She teaches courses in creative writing, literary nonfiction and environmental literature at Anne Arundel Community College in Maryland. She divides her time between Annapolis, Maryland, and Montauk, New York and is currently working on projects connecting her to both landscapes. She is editing an anthology of Chesapeake Bay Literature as well as working on a series of personal essays about Montauk, New York.

Rosemarie Rowley has published five books of poetry including *The Sea of Affliction* (1987) from which extracts are quoted in her essay. She has won the Epic award in the Scottish International Poetry Competition four times. Her most recent books are *Hot Cinquefoil Star* (2002) and *In Memory of Her.*

Allison Steele is a doctoral candidate at the University of Kentucky. Her research interests focus on ecocriticism, ecofeminism, and nineteenth century British literature.